THE JESUS PRAYER FOR TODAY

Arthur A. Vogel

The Jesus Prayer For Today

 PAULIST PRESS   New York/Ramsey

Library of Congress Catalog Card Number: 81-84349

ISBN: 0-8091-2413-0

Published by **Paulist Press,**
545 Island Road, Ramsey, N.J. 07446

Printed and bound in the United States of America

Contents

To my family

Preface

Waiting at an airport one day, I sat next to a young woman who casually began a conversation with me. Followers of the Guru Maharaj Ji had just concluded a convention in the city we were leaving, and the way she expressed herself, as well as her general manner, made me ask if she was a follower of the guru. She said that she was.

I asked if any other of the guru's disciples were in the crowd, and she replied that she was not sure, for she had not had time to look around. But she said she had found an almost foolproof way of identifying others who believed as she did: "I always look in the face; you can tell by the joy. It works wherever I am."

There should be something unmistakable in the lives of Christians, too. They should be known by their love, joy, and peace, and it is to help those who claim that Jesus is the Christ better to realize the consequences of their profession that these pages are written.

Christians ought to be recognized without any questions being asked.

Chapter I

The Time of Our Lives

Our concern is with the presence of God.

What could be more wonderful than to experience the presence of God in our lives?

We want to know and feel God's presence, but most frequently we want *our* God to be with us and so we desire the wrong God. We look for God's presence in our lives, but the way we search, judging from our success, seems best to prove that we use the wrong method to achieve our goal.

The basic religious problem for Christians should not be one of finding what is missing in their lives but one of discerning how God is already present in them. It is not our task to call Jesus "Lord" and then try to make him present; it is only because he is present that he is Lord!

The situation is well put in the First Letter of John: "We love, because he first loved us" (4:19). A few lines earlier in the same letter we read, "In this is love, not that we loved God but that he loved us and sent his Son to be the expiation for our sins" (4:10).

Christians profess that God sent his Son to be with them and that they can love God because he first loves them, but in spite of their profession they too frequently fail to know God's presence or his love in a compelling way. They talk about "presence" and "love," but in doing so they make ideas of both, removing them from time, and so removing them from the full reality of their lives. Jesus is not an idea; he is the Word of God, and a word spoken and uttered in time is very different from an idea standing outside time.

The first Christians were not so confused. They recognized God speaking directly to them in Jesus in a manner which not only took time but changed time. The ease with which Christians call Jesus "Christ" and go on to use the word "Christ" as if it were a proper name interchangeable with "Jesus" indicates two contrary things at the same time: the recognition of God in Jesus, which is the origin of Christianity, and the almost total loss of that same insight, which characterizes the lives of so many who call themselves Christian today.

"Christ," as is well known, means "Messiah," "the anointed one." When we call Jesus "Christ," we call him "Messiah," but more is involved in that equivalence than the interchangeability of two words. The recognition that Jesus is the Messiah is the insight from which Christianity was born, and it was the primal source of Christianity's early strength; the enfeebled state of Christians and Christianity today—the reason we do not know God's presence in our lives—is directly due to the fact that we do not know Jesus as the Christ.

Jews of Jesus' day were looking for a Messiah who would come to inaugurate his kingdom in the world. The establishment of the kingdom of the Messiah on earth meant that history would be fulfilled and along with it human existence. The end of time was expected with the coming of the Messiah, in the sense that the full meaning of time and the victory of God in time would be revealed. In fact, messianic expectation had begun to develop a twofold direction, one kingly and one priestly, at the time of Jesus. Life as the Jews lived it in their relations with the nations of the world and in their special relation to God as his chosen people gave content to the fulfillment anticipated in the Messiahs' coming.

The kingly Messiah was modeled on the royal line established by King David and was especially associated with the southern kingdom, Judah; the priestly Messiah was to be of the stock of Joseph and so was especially associated with the northern kingdom. In the oral tradition of the Jews, the priestly Messiah came to be called Ephraim; he was of the tribe of Levi, and it was further held that he would die and become a laughingstock and derision to all the world for the sake of his people.

Jesus could be seen by those who acknowledged him to be the Christ as the combination and fulfillment of both Messiahs. He came in time to fulfill time and to inaugurate a new time. The very fact of his coming into the world from the Father was the changing of time; to talk about him as "Christ" but to have his presence make no difference in the way we live time is to deny his having come into the world by the very title which is supposed to indicate that coming.

But is not such a contradiction between the way we live and the way we speak a good description of the difficulties we too frequently experience in trying to be Christian? The name by which we call ourselves often indicates what is most missing in our lives.

We may well know the difficulty we have just described, but what can we do about it? To admit that "Christ" means "Messiah" and that the first believers were Christians because they accepted Jesus as the Messiah does not in itself help us. If we are going to recognize the presence of God in Jesus in our lives today, must we develop the mentality of first-century Jews?

The answer is *no*; life in Christ leads us into the future, not into the past, and we are led into the future in the wholeness of our being, not just in a part of it. Jesus, in fact, fulfilled the messianic expectations of his day in a way which far surpassed the anticipation of the Messiah's coming. God's gift of himself is always more than any human anticipation of it; Jesus, although he was the Messiah, turned out to be very different from the Jewish expectation of him. The structure of messiahship, what the Messiah does for human existence in every place and time, rather than an historically limited description of the Messiah at a given time, is the important thing in the Messiah's coming.

When we think of the Jews anticipating the Messiah in their day, we must remember that, in the Mes-

4

siah's kingly dimension, their expectations were modeled on the glory of their nation in the time of David and Solomon; and, in the priestly dimension of the Messiah, uppermost in their minds was the history of the enslavement and redemption of their own people, culminating in the lives of Moses and the prophets. Jesus was recognized as the Messiah because he was seen to fulfill a unique relationship which had developed between God and his people Israel, but part of the unexpected nature of Jesus as Messiah in the Spirit was the bursting of Jewish nationalism by the new kingdom of God in Christ. Human fulfillment in Jesus, although entering the world through Judaism, was not limited to its Jewish roots. The entire human condition is changed by the Messiah's coming. No less a gift than a complete change in our being and in the way we live in the world is ours if we recognize Jesus to be the Christ.

Here we may turn again to our own religious struggles. Is it not fair to say that, as we strive to acquire the presence of God in our lives, we strive because we first feel something is missing in our lives? We begin with the recognition that all is not well with us; we think about our problems, and finally we turn to God as the one who can best meet our needs. In such a case, religion becomes an activity we add to other activities for the special use it can be to us. That a religion so acquired does not completely change our lives should not surprise us, for the core of our being remains untouched by the whole process. Such a religion is an activity in which we sometimes participate in our unchanged condition, rather than a gift of freedom which changes our condition.

When the Messiah comes, a new time of our lives, the End Time, comes with him. His time is called the End Time because in it the goal of time is achieved. The final victory of God in time is demonstrated and made available to us in a peace passing understanding. Time is filled with the presence of God and thus becomes our friend instead of our enemy.

What we have just said is summed up when Jesus is called "Christ." But is that the way Christians live today? Do we not act as though something was only begun in Jesus and as though more is yet to come? The difficulties we experience in our spiritual lives occur because we are obviously in greater need of what is yet to come than we are helped by what is already here.

But if that is true, God has not sufficiently completed his work in Jesus. And if that is true, Jesus is not the Christ, and if he is not, Christianity is a mistake and should lose its name.

We began with a problem—that of trying to recognize God's presence in our lives—and we have been led to another problem—that of whether or not Jesus really is the Messiah, the Christ. Concerning the latter problem, there are two possibilities: the basic problem can be either ours or God's. The problem is ours if Jesus is the Christ but we refuse to let him into our lives for who he is. It is God's problem if Jesus is the Christ but he is too weak to change our lives. Christians believe that God showed his almighty power in Jesus by victoriously raising him from the dead after his crucifixion; if that action of love has been truthfully related to us, there can be no doubt that God has the power to change our lives. If he were not thought to have the power to raise the dead, none of us would be bothering with him anyhow. That the problem is ours, not God's, is the only conclusion left to us.

Christianity has been itself through the ages because God has entered human lives and changed them in Jesus through the ages. If we accept the testimony of Jesus' having been raised from the dead, the reason we do not more convincingly show God's presence and love in our lives must be located in us rather than in God. Could it be that what we experience as the absence of God is actually our refusal to allow Jesus into our lives for who he really is? We talk about him as if he were an idea or a possibility, and in doing so we deny that he is the Christ who comes to us independently of us.

"Jesus," of course, is a proper name; it refers to a unique, distinct human being who once lived in the world. "Christ" means "anointed one"; it describes an abstract characteristic which could, at least theoretically, be applied to any number of people in the world. Following the usage of Paul, we have made a proper name of "Christ," using it as a synonym for "Jesus." The early Christian disciples, by making "Christ" a proper name, denied by that fact that the Messiah was a mere idea. To use "Christ" as a proper name was the most vivid way possible for people to proclaim that the End Time—the meaning of all time—had entered the world in Jesus of Nazareth. That is what the continued use of "Christ" as another name for Jesus down through the centuries should have proclaimed, but it often did not. In fact, the opposite seems frequently to have been the case. Instead of "Christ" being made concrete and specific by its application to Jesus, Jesus was made abstract and remote by being called "Christ."

To remove Christ from time is to destroy the meaning of "Messiah," and that is exactly what has happened for many people. Jesus is now thought to have come so long ago that he makes no difference in the present, and yet the only reason he was called "Christ" by the first disciples was because he was recognized to make a total difference in the world at every moment. He made a new way of living in the world possible, and so he inaugurated a new age.

The best Christians seem to be able to do today is to acknowledge that God once manifested his presence in a unique way in the world, when he sent his only-begotten Son into the world, and to acknowledge that God will uniquely come again, but this time with glory, in the second coming of the Son at some future time. Caught between the first and second comings, we feel we are presently in a valley looking backward and forward at two mountain peaks. Life in the valley lacks the perspective and exhilaration of life on the peaks, however, and for some people the peaks appear so distant that they are not sure whether they are seeing mountains or only cloud formations that will soon be blown away.

In the midst of the difficulties we encounter in trying to live Christian lives, we should question the adequacy of our expectations. Are we anticipating the right thing? Do we properly apprehend the nature of God's presence to us now? The second coming of Christ is commonly called the *parousia*, but the Greek word *parousia*, in itself, simply means "presence." The technical word for the End Time we have been talking about is *eschaton*: it comes from a Greek word meaning "last" or "end." As the two words have been used in Christian tradition and are most frequently used today, the parousia of Jesus is expected in the eschaton—and both of them are future. But the difficulties Christians are experiencing in their spiritual lives may come from precisely that fact. The presence of Jesus may be anticipated in the future in a manner which denies his presence now. Jesus can be pushed so completely into the past or into the future that he is of no real significance in the present. Yet as the Christ he is the one who brings the meaning of all time into the present.

In Jesus, God gives himself a history, living time as we live it where we live it. If Jesus truly is Lord, risen from the dead, he rules time now in order to be with us in the world today. There is no place but the present for us to live with God, so let us try to open ourselves to him in the manner of the first disciples, that is, in the new age inaugurated by Jesus as the Christ.

Chapter II

Christ's Time

We have said that because Jesus is present with us he is Lord. His presence is the proof of his title; his title does not make him present, as so many people know who apparently call him Lord in vain. Jesus is Lord because he is a living person now, not because he once was.

We have also remarked about how the presence of Jesus is confined to either the past or the future by many who call themselves Christian. As we look about, we do not see Jesus in the world today. We do not touch him or hear him. There were people who touched Jesus and saw him and heard him, however; they were his first disciples, the people whom he himself called to follow him. They have left us their testimony, and as that testimony was eventually written down we are able to read it in the New Testament. There is no doubt that a man named Jesus of Nazareth at one time lived in this world and walked on this earth.

A number of people who knew the man Jesus before his death experienced his presence with them after his death. They recognized his life in their lives—or their lives in his—and were convinced that God had won such a commanding victory in him that that victory would one day be manifest in the world with the same concreteness and visibility Jesus himself had before his death. Jesus would come again, and the difference between the first and second coming would not be in his visibility but in the glory which would be seen to belong to him. Such glory was not obvious in the world after Jesus' death, nor is it obvious today, and that absence emphasizes the absence of Jesus himself from the world.

The pictorially vivid manner in which the Gospel of Luke and the Acts of the Apostles describe the ascension of Jesus, for example, emphasize his absence from the world, even though Luke stresses the presence and gift of the Spirit after Christ's departure more vividly than does any other New Testament writer. In his Gospel, Luke has Christ carried up into heaven while in the act of blessing his disciples (24:51), and in the Acts of the Apostles, Luke once more has Christ lifted up into the sky until a cloud hides him from his disciples' sight. But once Christ is removed from sight two mysterious figures in white announce to the disciples that Jesus will come again in the same manner they had seen him go (1:6-11). Whether these descriptions of Jesus' departure are read literally or symbolically, the absence of Jesus from the world is the overwhelming impression with which the reader is left.

But that is not the message of the entire New Testament. If the description of Luke presents Christ ascending into heaven from his church, in a manner suggesting that we must await his coming again, the Gospel according to Matthew has the risen Christ coming to his people in order to remain with them until the completion of the age: "Go therefore and make disciples of all nations . . . and lo, I am with you always, to the close of the age" (28:19f.).

Jesus is Emmanuel, "God with us," in Matthew's Gospel (1:23), and the Gospel often recognizes the presence of Jesus in a manner different from his visual presence. Where two or three are gathered together in his name, Jesus is found in the midst of them (18:20). Jesus instructed his disciples that his presence is found in the hungry, thirsty, naked, imprisoned, or the stranger who was ministered to—or not—by them. "Truly, I say to you, as you did it to one of the least of these my brethren, you did it to me. . . . As you did it not to one of the least of these, you did it not to me" (25:31–45). Sending out the twelve Jesus said, "He who receives you receives me, and he who receives me receives him who sent me" (10:40). Jesus' mission in the world is universalized after his resurrection; that is why, as the Christ, he tells his followers to make disciples of all nations and promises to be with them always as they follow his command.

Although the end of Matthew's Gospel clearly states the presence of the risen Jesus with his people from the resurrection onward, in the community for which his Gospel was written there was still great emphasis laid on a future, second coming of Jesus which had not yet occurred. The Epistle to the Hebrews, on the other hand, sees the first coming of Jesus as an event in—or the inauguration of—the last days for which people had been waiting: "In many and various ways God spoke of old to our fathers by the prophets; but in these last days he has spoken to us by a Son, whom he appointed the heir of all things, through whom also he created the world" (1:1–2). Here we return to the affirmation that, since the Messiah comes only in the End Time, if Jesus is the Messiah, his presence ushers in the End Time.

The End Time is the time of fulfillment, not expectation. It is precisely as fulfilling time that the Gospel of Mark introduces Jesus as Christ, the Son of God (1:1), telling us that "after John was arrested, Jesus came into Galilee, preaching the gospel of God and saying, 'The time is fulfilled, and the kingdom of God is at hand; repent, and believe in the gospel'" (1:14–15).

It is in John's Gospel, however, that the meaning of Jesus' words, "Lo, I am with you always," is most intensely developed. The Gospel tells what the presence of Jesus means to believers in more detail and depth than any other; in it Jesus is seen as the Messiah and the time of Jesus is seen as the End Time. The presence of Christ dominates John's understanding of the last days. So it is that the End Time—and all the contents of the End Time—are present for John in Jesus. The presence of Jesus as Messiah brings all the ingredients of the End Time with him into the present.

The second coming of Christ and the final judgment of the world were two things expected by believers in the last days, but for John it is no longer necessary to wait for these events to occur. The presence of the living Christ to his people after the resurrection fulfills all past expectations and accomplishes all of God's plan. The resurrection enables Jesus to be with us in a now which lasts forever. We no longer fear a future judgment, and we no longer wait for anything which is missing. Judgment is accomplished; the Messiah has come; the final messianic age is here. The presence of Christ accomplishes all.

For John the expectation of a second coming of Jesus is fulfilled in the gift of the Spirit which occurred immediately after the resurrection. Speaking to his disciples before his death, Jesus tells them he will pray the Father to give them another Comforter, the Spirit, to be with them forever. Christ continues by saying, "I will not leave you desolate; I will come to you" (14:16–18). Clearly, Jesus is saying that *he* is made present in the gift of the Spirit. That promise is fulfilled in John as part of Jesus' post-resurrection appearances to his disciples, for, appearing to them as they were hiding on the first day of the week, he breathes on them and says, "Receive the Holy Spirit" (20:22). The gift of the Spirit is part of the great Easter event in John's telling of the good news; the bestowal of the Spirit indicates the glory of God committed to Jesus as the Christ. Earlier in John's Gospel we are told that "the Spirit had not yet been given, because Jesus was not yet glorified" (7:39). Jesus gives the Spirit after his resurrection because he has been glorified by his resurrection.

The clearest indication that John's community saw the presence of Christ himself to be the fulfillment of time and the coming of the kingdom of God is found in John's account of Jesus' discussion with Martha after the death of her brother Lazarus. Martha tells Jesus that she is sure her brother would not have died if Jesus had been there. Jesus replies that her brother will rise again. Martha responds, "I know that he will rise again in the resurrection at the last day." Jesus said to her, "I am the resurrection and the life. . . ." Asked whether she believed that statement, she said "Yes, Lord; I believe that you are the Christ, the Son of God, he who is coming into the world" (11:21–27).

When Martha begins her conversation with Jesus she expresses no more than an expectation held by many Jews of a resurrection of the dead at the last day. But John has Jesus tell her that what she expects in the future is already achieved in the present. The future has already come into her life. Jesus is not just an individual who needs to be resurrected; he is the spring of resurrection to which the thirsty come in death. He is not one individual among others waiting for resurrection. He is the *resurrection*: he is the new time, the new epoch, for which people have been waiting. His presence defines the End Time. When Martha recognizes that, she recognizes him to be the Messiah for whom she and her people had been waiting.

The presence of Jesus, we have seen, is also the presence of judgment according to John. The End Time was thought by the Jews to be the time of judgment for the world, and when the End Time is postponed to some future time, so is the final judgment postponed. But when the End Time is present, so is judgment, and that is exactly what John announces. Anticipating his death, Jesus says in John's Gospel,

"*Now* is the judgment of this world" (12:31). John consistently carries out the implications of recognizing Jesus to be the Messiah, but although John also has Jesus say, "For judgment I came into this world" (9:39), John understands God's purpose in sending his Son into the world to be salvation rather than judgment. God is love, and "God so loved the world that he gave his only Son, that whoever believes in him should not perish but have eternal life. For God sent the Son into the world, not to condemn the world, but that the world might be saved through him" (3:16-17).

When the presence of Jesus becomes the source of condemnation, it is because people condemn and judge themselves. "He who believes in him is not condemned; he who does not believe is condemned already, because he has not believed in the name of the only Son of God. And this is the judgment, that the light has come into the world, and men loved darkness rather than light, because their deeds were evil" (3:18–19). Lovers of darkness judge themselves in the presence of light. Jesus brings judgment because he is the presence of light.

The new covenant God makes with his people— the New Testament, as we usually refer to it—is based on the recognition that Jesus is the Messiah. Once that recognition is made, however, the different communities within which the books of the New Testament were written understood the role of the Messiah differently. Some, although calling Jesus "Messiah" in the present, almost immediately reverted to the normal Jewish expectation of the period and projected his truly effective coming into the future. Others, such as the community of John, emphasized his presence as

16

Messiah now, and so found all the elements of the End Time in the present.

The situation we have just described is more than just an interesting insight about the nature of New Testament communities. We are participants in the same act of decision which faced them, for we face the same alternatives and ambiguities which the New Testament Church faced. In fact, they are even more acute with us. Jesus' victory is not clear in the eyes of the world; thus, if we accept Jesus as the Christ, there is good reason for believing that his most compelling coming still lies in the future. On the other hand, if he truly is the Messiah, and he has come into the world, then the End Time, which the Jews anticipated with the coming of the Messiah, must be present with him. In the presence of Jesus, the future is now.

There are difficulties either way. If Jesus' second coming is projected into the future, we may ask when he will come again. Will he ever come? So many people have expected his second coming at so many different times in the two thousand years of Christianity's existence, and have read so many signs of the times wrongly, that we may wonder whether or not he will ever come again. After all, disappointment after disappointment, error after error, for centuries does not breed confidence. The other alternative has difficulties also. If the End Time is now, the presence of Jesus with us in it is so different from our expectations that we appear to miss it altogether.

What are we to do?

Jesus is either present or he is not; if he is present, *he* is here for who he is no matter what theories we hold about him. If Jesus is present to us as the Christ—

as the Messiah—can he bring anything with him other than the End Time and the type of living that time requires? Everything depends on whether we recognize him as Messiah or not. But we must remember that it is only as Messiah that he is claimed to have risen from the dead and to be present with us, for he is called "Christ."

Let us not forget that there were many in Jesus' day who did not recognize him to be the Christ. He was not the kind of Messiah people expected. Is it possible that his coming in glory has already begun and that we are missing it for the same reason non-believers missed the first coming—it is not what we expect?

The Messiah is associated with glory, but non-believers in Jesus' day missed God's glory in the cross. They did not know the glory of love. The Spirit is consistently identified with God's glory and power in Scripture, but we miss the glory of the coming of Christ in the Spirit because we, too, do not know the glory of love! A certain consistency is discovered in the refusal human beings make to God's advances. Perhaps we are not so different from the first non-believers; perhaps we are doing the same thing today they did then, only they did it to deny that Jesus was the Christ, and we do it in the name of a Christianity which denies that Jesus is the Christ.

We want to anticipate a future second coming of Christ because, as commonly understood, at that coming God will do everything. He will act and set things right, and our passive faith will be rewarded by his action. Our pretense of remaining pure so that we will deserve our reward is our greatest betrayal of the

Christ who has come, and so it is the judgment we make upon ourselves.

We act as if Christ's second coming will be his first coming. We spend our time talking about something and anticipating something that will be real, instead of acknowledging that Christ has come and accepting him in our lives in the fullness with which he has come into the world. We do not accept him under the guise of waiting for him—and yet it is only because he has already come as Christ that we know it is he for whom we are waiting! We will do anything to keep doing nothing, to keep from accepting Jesus' presence now.

Now is the final judgment, for Jesus is the full revelation of the Father (Col. 1:15, 19); we judge ourselves by refusing to accept him as Christ. The parousia, the presence of Christ, is already accomplished in the gift of the Spirit. The End Time is now. Everything is not yet over, however, for we rightly anticipate a future in which the full consequences of the second coming will be plain, but no new revelation of God will be brought into the world. The love we already know in Jesus, and which already indwells us in the Spirit, is the love which triumphs.

The Jews believed that before the Christ appeared the antichrist would come as additional testimony that the End Time had arrived. Since Jesus' day there have been many candidates for the role of the antichrist in human history, yet because the second coming has not begun in the manner generally thought by people to be appropriate for it, candidate after candidate for the role of antichrist has been denied the title. The First Letter of John, in general agreement with the thought of John's Gospel, does not yield to such opinions. The letter unhesitatingly states: "Children, it is the last hour. . . . Who is the liar but he who denies that Jesus is the Christ? This is the antichrist, he who denies the Father and the Son" (2:18, 22). The antichrist is anyone who denies that Jesus is the Christ. If the author of the letter is correct, expectations about the coming of the Christ have been fulfilled, but the fulfillment has once more been different than had been expected. The problem, we discover again, is ours instead of God's.

In the End Time we are simply to live Christ's presence in the Spirit. No more is possible. The effect of Christ's presence will become more full in the future; what is here already will become more evident, but nothing new will come. Our lack of faith, not Christ's absence, is what is holding things up.

When the presence of Jesus in these last days is accepted everywhere, the second coming, which has now begun, will be completed and the new will have completely overcome the old. The kingdom of God will then be consummate on earth. Because we are living in the End Time, there is nothing we need be anxious about. All we have to do is to show what has come into the world rather than obscure it. Since love has come, we can abide in love (Jn. 15:9); since peace has come, we can abide in peace (Jn. 14:27). If we are waiting for the last days to come in a still-distant future, as many people have been waiting for century after century, trying to abide in the Son's love in the present world will seem to be an unsupported task with a never-ending goal. The fact is that in the presence of the risen Jesus through the power of the Spirit, the future has already come into the present, as Martha realized. In Christ the End Time is *now*. We are already living in the intimate presence of God which never ends.

Chapter III

Faith Is Openness to God

We live in the End Time, we have said, because Jesus has come to us as the Messiah, the Christ. The presence of Jesus as Christ is the crucial factor. If we do not actually experience his presence in our lives, he remains no more than an idea or a name. If we experience his presence, our lives will proclaim his lordship.

Words by themselves remain inadequate.

There is no method for learning love, because love overflows methods. Love is a total relationship between persons; we love God because he first loved us, as St. John has reminded us. The Christian life is our response in the Spirit to the love God has shown for us in Christ, but that response is not calculated. The most difficult thing about the Christian life is its simplicity. To be Christian we must do nothing more than let Jesus love us. It takes time for that to happen, however, and we are in a hurry to use religion for our purposes.

It is not enough just to admit that God loves us,

or, after acknowledging his love, planning our strategy for carrying his love into the world. We do not carry his love; his love carries us. Sooner or later ultimate reality must show in our lives for what it is, and in Christianity that showing is sooner rather than later.

We can never know God's love unless we let him love us first. Love always moves first; that is the only way it can be itself. It is just a matter of whether we want to try to extend our efforts to God or whether we are willing to let God's love into our lives. In the latter case something new happens to us; in the former case things remain basically the same.

If we will let God love us first, we will find that tasks we have to perform and obligations we once dreaded are not places we will have to search for God; instead they will be places God finds us. Jesus is sent by the Father to be with us. He comes independently of our effort and is already with us before we undertake anything. To try to find him is already to have lost him. "Father, you send your Son to me," is our first recognition of the God who is Love.

Our only concern must be to remain open to God. The dare we receive from God is to accept nothing less than the love he offers us in his Son. "Openness to God" is a good way of defining faith, and another name for such openness is "prayer." Faith and prayer are means by which the presence of God in Christ fills our lives, enabling us to live in a manner appropriate to Christ's time. We will say something about Christian faith in a few moments, and we will examine a traditional form of prayer, which can be especially helpful to us in living with Jesus as the Messiah, in a few chapters.

In Jesus the mystery of God entered our world, and Jesus' resurrection is our assurance of God's ability to carry us beyond ourselves to himself in love. Because such love breaks into our lives with a power beyond our comprehension, sharing the life of God, not just talking about it, is the important thing. Knowledge of God as an object does nothing for us and neither does such knowledge of his Son. Because Christ's resurrected life is different from life in this world, the resurrection cannot be known and described as if it were an object of this world. Yet in the practice of our religion we keep trying to equate the resurrection with what it cannot be—a mere past event—and ignoring what it must be—the living Jesus present to us at this moment. We keep trying to reduce God and his acts to what we can understand from our point of view, thereby denying God's mystery and trying to reduce his personal presence to worldly nonsense. We prefer to keep the resurrection in the past and to anticipate it in the future; and then, as we know, it has no power in the present.

The truth of the matter is that convincing proof of the resurrection can be found only in the living Jesus himself; memories of him or stories about him, even if true, will not do. The resurrection of Jesus does not mean that something odd, and something which remains in the past, happened centuries ago. It means instead that Jesus is alive now and that he offers us his life to live right here because he is the Christ. Only if we are able to live his resurrected life as our own can we know with certainty that he is not dead.

The resurrection of Jesus cannot be known as if it were one object among others in the world; the resurrection is too wonderful for that. But it must nevertheless be possible for us to know the reality of Jesus' resurrection in our own lives, or Christianity is no better than a fable. Even if the resurrection once took place, but Jesus lived after it only to be absent from us in the present, his victory would be his defeat. So God makes it possible for us to confirm the victory of Christ in our lives today. The God who comes to us in Jesus is a redeemer, someone who changes things; he is not content merely to have a fact recorded about him in the record books. He comes to change us, not to put on a display before us.

But a lingering doubt persists. How, we ask, are we able to experience the resurrection victory of Christ? How do we get his life into ours? We want to be people of faith, but is our act of faith an act of courage alone, an act in which we summon up all of our will power, take a chance on Jesus, and then wait to see what happens? We know that living by faith is different from living by sight, and we know that faith can transport us to realms beyond the reach of our natural abilities, but is there any support for our faith? Is there nothing but the words of others to sustain our faith in Jesus, if he has risen from the dead?

The answer to these questions is found in the realization that to have faith in Jesus is not to stand alongside him and hope that we can become like him. For a Christian, to have faith in Jesus is nothing less than to live the faith of Jesus; such intimacy is what the resurrected Jesus brings into our lives.

That we are able to live the faith of Jesus helps us to understand some words of Paul which are classic words of Christian commitment, but which, because of the total commitment they require, have perhaps discouraged more people than they have helped. Paul wrote in his Letter to the Galatians: "I have been crucified with Christ; it is no longer I who live, but Christ who lives in me; and the life I now live in the flesh I live by faith in the Son of God, who loved me and gave himself for me" (2:20). People read this passage seeking the consolation of Christ's living in them, but the consolation they desire is frequently denied by the thought of having to be crucified with Christ. Actually, Paul is not describing a temporal sequence of events in the words we have quoted. From the point of view of time, the thing Paul mentions last happens first: before anything is asked of us, God first loves us and gives himself for us. God's presence in our lives transforms our lives, and only after such change occurs do we live differently.

Paul says the life he lives in the flesh he lives "by faith in the Son of God." The Greek text more literally reads: "The life I now live in the flesh I live by [the] faith of the Son of God. . . ." Paul, then, is claiming that the life he lives in the world is the faith—the very openness to God—of Jesus who loved him and gave himself for him. Since the love given to Paul was the love shown on the cross, by living the openness to God of the triumphant Jesus, Paul, too, lives the openness of love shown on the cross. That is how he is crucified with Christ and why such crucifixion is his consolation.

We seldom think of Jesus as a man of faith because, as Son of God, faith seems to be unworthy of him. He is God, but he is also, we must remember, truly human. As a human being, Jesus lived life under exactly the same conditions we do; otherwise he could not save us. Faith is openness to God, and it is because Jesus is perfectly open to God that he is the person of perfect faith.

When we are called to faith in Jesus, we are not called to something about which we can only read in books or hear about from others. We are not left to imitate something which happened centuries ago. The resurrection of Jesus from the dead means that his openness to the Father is offered to us as our openness to God now, at this very moment. Our faith is not the unsupported chance that we can be like someone who died thousands of years ago. In the final analysis, it would be absurd to want to be like someone who had been dead so long.

We can have first-hand knowledge that Jesus is risen from the dead to the extent that we live *his* openness to the Father in his Spirit. The living of that openness is how he is present to us now. Our faith is not meant to be an imitation of Jesus' faith, it is meant to be the faith of Jesus. Open to Christ in faith, we are open to the Father in Christ. Jesus himself is then the support of our faith; we do not believe alone. Living Jesus' faith, his openness, at this moment when he is also living it victoriously as Lord of heaven and earth, is our experience of his resurrection. Since he is alive, his faith sustains us, opening us to the Father. The living of Jesus' faith is how he lives in us and we in him. His faith in us is the gift of the Spirit to us, the gift of his glory while we are still in this life.

To live the faith of Jesus is to know that everything is all right. It is to trust God and to be free for God's service in the world. In the faith of Jesus made present in us by the Spirit we are surrounded by the power of God, the power which has already raised Jesus from the dead and enabled his faith to become ours. There is nothing to do—our arms are held up by another and our lives are supported by God's presence. The Messiah has come; his victory is ours to live.

Chapter IV

Mystery Brought Close

Because he is sent from God, the Messiah is a mysterious person.

God is Mystery—beyond everything, yet not nothing.

Infinite Mystery is the Source and End of all. What is such Mystery like? How can we refer to it personally? God's boundless depth and difference cannot be described. God casts no shadow, makes no sound, yet his power is everywhere. He comes from nothing; he gives all. How can he be Source? Certainly he is beyond the distinction of male and female, as he is beyond every distinction found in his creation.

God is beyond our capacity adequately to fear or love; our full awe of him cannot fully acknowledge him, for he is the concentration of Reality too intense for our fragile being. Because he is Mystery, everything we know is surrounded and sustained by mystery. We know there is more around us than we see, and in our better moments we admit that we do not fully know what we see. Mystery is found within our world as well as beyond it.

Our being is mysterious too, for we come from God and somehow are made in his image. Our mystery recognizes Mystery and longs for fulfillment in it.

But questions remain. Events in the world do not illustrate a simple theory. For what purpose is our life on earth? Is it right to spend so much effort on something which lasts such a short time? How can so many people be wrong if some are right? Can everyone be wrong? Is our life an exercise in nonsense? Why does suffering exist? How are those who suffer selected? Are they selected? If they are not selected, why are they abandoned? Are they abandoned? We must depend on Something beyond us but what is that Something and how should we relate to it?

The distinctive claim made for Jesus is that he is the Word of Mystery calling us to himself. He does not tell us why things are as they are. He comes to take us deeper into Mystery.

Jesus, we have indicated, is the mystery of God living in our world. We need a Jesus with breadth, depth, power, presence and challenge. Jesus, the Messiah, raised from the dead, makes even a cosmic difference. A Jesus naively believed in, someone who is asked to meet broad human needs in a narrow way, will not do. Christians should not tolerate a Jesus invoked against a full awareness of the world.

Jesus a scandal, yes, but an embarrassment, no!

Jesus is the sacred name hallowed by God himself, not the label owned by an enthusiast.

Jesus is as strong as the power of the resurrection;

he is, in fact, the power of the resurrection. There is a sense in which the Spirit is the power of the resurrection, but the sole work of the Spirit is to make Jesus present.

Trying to live *by* the power of the resurrection is different from living the power of the resurrection. The power of the resurrection is more than power itself; it is the presence of Jesus. "Power" alone is unfinished. It is energy which can be used a number of different ways, and we want to be the ones to direct its use according to our wills. But the power of the resurrection is not a bundle of energy God gives us to use in any way we want; the power is God's and he has already used it the way he wants. It is the power of love, the presence of Jesus. That is why Jesus could say, "I am the resurrection" (Jn. 11:25).

The Son of God is able to be absolute in our lives because he is a mystery. What is fully intelligible to us is exhaustible by us. What we can understand we can make commonplace, but a mystery we confront while not comprehending is consuming. A true mystery refreshes us precisely because of its inexhaustibility; it nourishes, intrigues, and absorbs us by its presence.

The fully mysterious is something we live within rather than just live by, and only because the Christ is such a mystery can we live "in Christ," as Paul put it. Mystery is more than we are. It draws us in our fullness into itself.

It is not what we do not know about Jesus that makes him mysterious, but what we know. Jesus is God's way of sharing his mystery with us. The seer who wrote the Book of Revelation knew that truth well. He tells us that in the course of his vision he saw

31

heaven open and a white horse appear. The one who sat upon the horse was called Faithful and True; besides those names the rider was called "The Word of God," and a short time later we are also told that "on his robe and on his thigh he has a name inscribed, King of kings and Lord of lords." But even those names do not exhaust the identity of the rider, for in addition to the names known to us "he has a name inscribed which no one knows but himself" (Rev. 19:11-16).

As difficult as the Book of Revelation is to decipher from time to time, there is no difficulty in admitting that its author had a deep and profound understanding of Jesus as the Son of God. No proof of that fact is needed beyond the words we have just quoted. In the vision we have recounted, Jesus is seen coming to us as Word of God, as King of kings, and as Lord of lords, and yet he has another name which only he knows. Jesus is God speaking to us, and he is King and Lord, but even when he is so recognized he is a mysterious Word, a mysterious King, and a mysterious Lord. Even when we hear the Word of God, who among us fully understands it? We rejoice to hear the Word, but we do not master it. The Word is our master; that is why it saves us. We receive it, but we do not comprehend it. That the God whom no created person can ever understand loves us and takes us to himself is the source of our exaltation. Mystery is our life.

Jesus is uniquely identified with God; God's own Spirit dwells in him and makes him different from everyone else. In the Bible the Spirit of God is identified with God's mystery as well as with his glory. The

Spirit is the mysterious depth of the unseen God. To be able to understand the Spirit would be to understand God, but no one can do that. The Spirit, as the invisible wind to the primitive, moves at its will independently of us.

Mark's Gospel begins with the proclamation that Jesus is the Son of God and explicitly and repeatedly associates the Spirit of God with Jesus for that reason. John the Baptist says that the Son will not baptize with water as John does, but with the Holy Spirit. When Jesus is baptized by John, he sees the Spirit descending upon him; then we read that the Spirit drove Jesus into the wilderness; and after teaching with an astonishing authority in the synagogue at Capernaum, a man possessed by an unclean spirit identifies Jesus as the "Holy One of God" (Mk. 1:1–24). Jesus is the Holy One of God because the Holy Spirit dwells within him.

Luke's Gospel associates the Spirit with Jesus even more elaborately. John the Baptist, the one who will prepare the way for the Lord, will be filled with the Holy Spirit according to the angel's message to Zechariah, John's father; Mary is told that the Holy Spirit will come upon her; Elizabeth, John's mother, is filled with the Holy Spirit to say that the fruit of Mary's womb is blessed; Simeon was inspired by the Spirit to say that he had seen the salvation God prepared for his people when he saw the child Jesus; and, as in Mark, Luke tells of the Spirit descending on Jesus at his baptism, has Jesus filled by the Spirit and led by the Spirit into the wilderness, and finally has Jesus return from his temptation "in the power of the Spirit" (Lk. 1–4).

Jesus is the mystery of God with us, mystery intensified by being in our midst, not mystery diluted or domesticated by its nearness. "Christ," as we have seen, means "the anointed one," and to call Jesus the Christ is to say that he has been especially anointed with the Spirit of God. Recognizing Jesus as the Christ is a way of tracing the identity of Jesus back to God, the Unknown, for Jesus' anointing with the Spirit is God's sovereign action.

We must not let intimacy be reduced to familiarity. If intimacy with Jesus is reduced to familiarity with him, then he is lost to us as Lord and Savior, the Son of God. In Jesus, God brought the mystery of himself closer to us, let it live among us, let us live with—even in—it; in Jesus, God showed us what his mystery is, but he did not explain his mystery away. Jesus is God living among us as a human being, but God did not become understandable by that fact. If anything, God became more mysterious by his presence in Jesus, not less, for no God we can understand could do such a thing as God did in Jesus. If we accept Jesus as the Son of God, his very intimacy with us magnifies the mystery of God in our lives. The closeness of Jesus intensifies God's mystery for us, for in Jesus we can live God's mystery as our life.

God became human in Jesus so we could have a personal encounter with him. As overworked as the word "encounter" has become recently, what it describes is the basis of our life in Christ. Genuine Christianity is nothing less than a personal encounter with God in Jesus. Because, when we live as Christians, we live in the presence of Jesus as a person, there is always a wholeness—his wholeness—in our lives. Our

Christian lives begin when the wholeness of Jesus is given to us, and all of our growth occurs within that wholeness. We cannot grow into the wholeness from the outside. Christian growth occurs only within Christ, because outside Christ nothing is Christian. Jesus alone is Messiah, the one sent from God.

Chapter V

Christian Sophistication

"No one can know God without knowing Jesus, and no one can know Jesus without knowing God." Those words have been offered as the true meaning of accepting Jesus as the Son of God. They tell what it means to believe that Jesus is God Incarnate.

The words are the charter of Christianity.

They are more than a charter in the abstract sense, however; to know their truth is to live as a Christian.

The words we have quoted state neither a truism nor a self-evident maxim. They are a way of admitting total dependence on Jesus; they are a way of saying that God has taken our search for him out of our hands and given himself to us his way. We profess that if we want to know God there is no alternative to Jesus.

To acknowledge the words as a statement about Christianity is easy enough. To accept the words as the truth of our lives, on the other hand, is to find a radical demand being made of us. Most people, even those who say they are Christian, seem to miss the absolute nature of the words, for the words claim that Jesus is an absolute. Actually Jesus is the Absolute come to us, and until he is absolute in our lives we do not know him as the Messiah.

For Christians there can be no alternative to Jesus. That, as we have indicated, is what the words we have quoted mean, but that is not the way people want to interpret them. "Interpretation" is the key, and here we find ourselves led to confront a basic issue of Christian faith. Is Christianity an interpretation of life or total dependence on Jesus? There is less risk in the former alternative from the intellectual point of view, but there is less risk in the latter if we need a Savior.

Words so frequently are our problem. They are the distinctive means of human communication. The sciences, the arts, and the different cultures of the world are exercises in using different systems of words. But is religion no more than a matter of words, a way of talking about the world? There are too many words in the world, and they save no one. We need someone who will save his words and save us. We need release and freedom which words alone do not bring into our lives—not even the right words. "For the kingdom of God does not consist in talk but in power" (1 Cor. 4:20).

But isn't accepting Jesus as Absolute too much?

Actually, only is it enough if the distinction between an interpretation of life and a Savior is understood. To accept Jesus as one who brings a special interpretation of life to us is to accept him as no more than another person entering into the on-going debate about human life. He becomes another Socrates and the cross is no more than his form of hemlock. He becomes another human being of good intention who is killed by those who find life easier with him out of their way. But his enemies found they could not completely destroy him, for after his death his views lived on in the minds of others.

As people are born into the world and become participants in the dialogue of life, some become convinced that Jesus' opinions remain the best they can find, while others become convinced that other religious leaders and philosophers offer better options.

But a person who accepts the interpretation of life offered by Jesus as the best way to live is not yet a Christian. Jesus is more than the words he used, and life in him does not consist in quoting him. Life in Jesus is not the best way to live but the only way for a Christian. That is what it means to say that we cannot know God without knowing Jesus and cannot know Jesus without knowing God.

Jesus is the Way.

Jesus' life is not an organizing principle; it is a source of blessing. Only for that reason could he utter the beatitudes, giving a completely new meaning to human life in them. The beatitudes given in the Sermon on the Mount turn human life upside down; they are impossible rules to follow if they are thought to be no more than abstract ethical principles Jesus advocated as the means of personal fulfillment. Empty of Jesus' personal presence as the Christ, the beatitudes *are* foolishness. When received in Jesus' presence, on the other hand, they become marks of human liberation and freedom rather than enslaving rules too difficult to follow. Nor are the beatitudes campaign promises made to attract followers by promising people a happy life in heaven no matter how dreadful their lives are on earth. The beatitudes are not just statements that the poor in spirit, those who mourn, the meek, those who hunger and thirst for righteousness, the merciful, the pure in heart, the peacemakers, and those who are persecuted will have a better life in the future because of their troubles now.

The beatitudes are ways of saying that Jesus is the only source of blessing we know and that, in Jesus, God is present even in what appear to be the most vulnerable dimensions of human life, turning weakness into strength. The conditions described by the beatitudes are conditions in which anyone can recognize the need for help beyond himself. The beatitudes state that if we recognize our needs in Jesus, he, the Christ, becomes our help from the moment of our recognition on.

Because Jesus is the one mysteriously anointed with the Spirit, there is no alternative to him. He comes to call us to God, for in him God says something to us and does something for us he says and does no place else. Jesus' significance is not distributed throughout creation in a way we can discover by ourselves. He is not a truth we uncover; he is *the* truth enlightening us.

Jesus is the love of God breaking human comprehension. Christian maturity consists in seeing a great principle which is lost if it is reduced to no more than a principle. A person mature in Christ knows that the mysterious God who reveals himself in the mysterious Christ cannot be reduced to an abstract principle.

Christian maturity brings a special kind of sophistication, and it takes that sophistication to relate to God in Jesus. There is a radical difference in the way God expresses himself to us as a human being and the way we human beings try to express ourselves as God.

Christian sophistication understands that God comes to us so completely in Jesus that we must be our whole selves in accepting him. We must accept him as he comes, not as we prefer him in our thinking. The mystery of God must constrain us instead of being emptied by us. His wisdom is different from ours. His wisdom forces change—that is why it is our redemption; our wisdom justifies the way things are, for our wisdom is the product of the way things are. Human wisdom reduces God to our level: we try to reduce God's action to our understanding by elevating our understanding to God's action. God's wisdom overcomes us. "For Christ did not send me to baptize but to preach the Gospel, and not with eloquent wisdom, lest the cross of Christ be emptied of its power. For the word of the cross is folly to those who are perishing, but to us who are being saved it is the power of God .... For since, in the wisdom of God, the world did not know God through wisdom, it pleased God through the folly of what we preach to save those who believe. For Jews demand signs and Greeks seek wisdom, but we preach Christ crucified, a stumbling block to Jews and folly to Gentiles, but to those who are called, both Jews and Greeks, Christ the power of God and the wisdom of God. For the foolishness of God is wiser than men, and the weakness of God is stronger than men" (1 Cor. 1:17–25).

We are constantly tempted to accept Jesus as less

than absolute in our lives. Our temptation about Jesus is much the same as Jesus' temptation about the Father. As the Gospel according to Matthew recounts Jesus' first temptation, "the tempter came and said to him, 'If you are the Son of God, command these stones to become loaves of bread.' But he answered, 'It is written, "Man shall not live by bread alone, but by every word that proceeds from the mouth of God"'" (Matt. 4:3f). Jesus' temptation was to use God as the means of answering his human needs; it was the temptation to be religious for his reasons, not God's. We know the temptation well. We, too, have needs, and we are aware of the continuing temptation of letting God into our lives only to the extent that he answers our requests. Our needs can be offered to Jesus, but they cannot rule him, for he is absolute. Living in him we become different and, once different, our needs change. That is the paradox stated in the beatitudes. In Jesus the poor are rich; that is not to say that the penniless are lucky—it is to say that even if one has money he is rich only in Jesus.

Chapter VI

Authority and Power

When we recognize that God loves us first by entering our lives in Jesus, things begin to change for us. Jesus' victory over death is his way, as the Christ, of claiming this world for his kingdom and of establishing his time, the End Time, as the time of our lives. The Messiah makes a difference, and how different the difference is when the difference is Jesus!

Strange as it might sound at first, Jesus cannot be proclaimed as if he were the best answer to the problems of our lives. If we argue that Jesus is the best answer to our problems, we may not convince others, for they may claim to have better answers for themselves than we do. Humility requires that we not be too sure about what we recommend to them. To argue that Jesus is the best among other possibilities reduces him to one option among many in the world. It is to take an apologetic approach to him and make him no more effective than our arguments for him; it is to compromise his nature as the Christ.

Actually, Jesus is not the best answer to our problems; he is the only answer. He is the only way to the Father. At least that is the Christian view, and, on that view, the odd consequence follows that we do not have to judge other people and their answers. God will take care of that. All we have to do is proclaim Jesus as we know him. We are witnesses, not judges.

We can spend our whole lives trying to show that religion is reasonable, and so miss Jesus, for he is not reasonable! He is a person with an actuality of his own; he cannot—and does not—wait for us and our theories to let him be himself.

The scandal of Christianity is not just the kind of Messiah Jesus turned out to be, but that, since Jesus has come, there is no other Way. We cannot expand or generalize the scandal and see the truth of Jesus anywhere else. Jesus alone is Son of God.

There is no means by which we can make Jesus real by ourselves; there is no way we can own him, and no method will enable us to command him. He comes to us as the Christ too immediately for our means and methods to have any effect. To want to meet him our way is to want to control him, to want to limit and specify his role in our lives. It is to keep him, in other words, from being himself. He comes to us breaking our expectations apart—just as he shattered the expectations of the Jews of his day; he even breaks our needs apart. If he only fulfills our needs, we remain our old selves.

Because the Christ frees us from ourselves, trying

to use ourselves as guides to him is the one sure way of avoiding him. Even our anticipation of his acting in a new way is a fetter we prepare for him. We may throw a trap into the woods not knowing where it will land, but it is still our trap.

Jesus is someplace and he is someone. He is specific and definite in himself. But what he is where he is always is something we know only within his presence. He is the Word of God who initiates every conversation with us. The fact that he moves first and calls us beyond ourselves is our liberation as we live in response to him, but such calling is our insecurity and fear as we anticipate it by ourselves. The truth is that we are dislocated without Jesus no matter where we are and no matter how familiar our surroundings may be. It is because his presence always calls us beyond ourselves that we cannot have him for our comfort only within ourselves. Everything he offers us—freedom, peace, love, security—is a relation to him, not a quality which is ours to keep and which we can use or ignore as we wish.

To be with Jesus is not to rest in a state. His freedom is a demand, not a refuge. In Jesus we do not dread what tomorrow will bring; in Jesus we do not even need to know what will happen tomorrow, for if we are with Jesus we will always be beyond ourselves no matter where we are. That is Christian peace. Such peace is not a state to be preserved unchanged; it is not a breath to hold. To try to keep Jesus with us as something static from the past is actually to be alone. He is a walking companion, and he walks with us into the future.

When Jesus said, "Peace I leave with you; my

peace I give to you" (Jn. 14:27), he did not give his peace to us as something to keep in our possession and use only on occasion, as if receiving his peace were different from using it. Jesus' peace is a relation to God and is given only in its use. It is an actuality instead of a potentiality, for it is God's gift. Peace is the presence of Jesus as Messiah; as Jesus is present or absent, so is his peace. Neither Jesus nor his peace comes without the other—and they leave together.

We all want authority in our lives even though we live in an age which is generally anti-authoritarian.

To live with authority means to live with sureness and security, something everyone seeks but few find. Pension funds are one attempt to find security, but inflation is the pin which pricks the golden bubble.

I met a young man once who was rebelling against the religion of his youth. He told me the name of the church he had gone to, and he told me that he had been well trained in religion, as had everyone who had been a continuing member of the congregation. He knew when to stand and when to kneel and how to find his place in the prayer book; he said that he, like every youngster who grew up in the parish, knew exactly what he could do and what he could not do from the religious point of view in almost every aspect of his life. There were rules in religion, and he had been taught the rules. Although he had been well trained as he grew up and became more independent and left home, he said his religion was no help at all. "It was very authoritarian, but it had no authority," as he put it.

It is not just that we need authority in our lives; authority can be used destructively as well as creatively. Jesus himself talked about the rulers of the Gentiles exercising lordship over them, and his point was that Christian authority should not be exercised that way.

Not just authority, but *God's* authority is what we long for in the uncertainties of the world. To live by God's authority is to be liberated and freed from the world while we are in the world. To have God's authority in our lives is to live with such assurance that we know a peace the world cannot destroy.

It is not surprising that we need authority in our lives when we remember that the Greek word for authority is also a word for *power*. No argument is needed to convince us that power is good for us; power is what everyone is fighting for—and with. In the life of Christ, his resurrection from the dead was the consuming manifestation of power, but, as we read the Gospels, it was the authoritative way Jesus forgave sins which was the first indication of the unique power dwelling in him. The authority to forgive sins was the power to forgive sins; whether Jesus had such power was the primary source of controversy about him. As Christians accept Jesus today, they know that the power by which he overcame death is the power by which he forgives sin. The former is the proof of the latter. The power which overcame death is the power which forgives sin, for, as we shall discuss in more detail later, sin *is* death. Sin, just like death, is isolation from God.

Knowing that God comes to us in power and offers his power to us, how can we accept it? By accepting forgiveness. That is the way to live by his authority, the way to get his authority into our lives. Once again, Christianity presents a paradox to the world. Those who want ultimate power can acquire it only by accepting forgiveness. It all makes good sense if Jesus is the Word of God spoken with power, but it does not make much sense in the words of the world.

To proclaim the authority of Christ in our lives is not to enter a battle of ideas with those who think differently than we do; it is rather to live a life that is bigger than ideas—even ideas about Christ. Christ's authority is not something to be kept in mind. It cannot be kept in mind at all, for it is not an idea. Christian dialogue with others is not the nimble display of ideas, but the service of others in love.

Ideas do not exist in time; they abstract so completely from the full conditions of human life that they do not grow old, decay, or change at all. Although ideas do not die, they are not immortal either, for they do not live. People live, and it is they who have ideas. The authority of an idea is restricted to other ideas; we all know that thought alone does not control life. People freeze to death while thinking of fire, and the things we have left undone which we ought to have done are usually things we have at least thought about.

If authority is to be fully significant in our lives, it must be an authority which exists in time and which works through time, even controlling time. *Persons* have ultimate authority for us, and if a person is someone who has authority over me, or is someone I recognize as an authority, he or she makes a difference to me now. If I recognize Jesus as the Christ, he must make a difference to me now. If Jesus is the Christ, he makes a difference to me in time, through time, not behind or beyond time. To live Christ's authority is the only way to relate to it; living is the only way his authority can show, for his authority is his life. He came and gave himself—his life—for us. He did not come merely to talk about himself and ask us to go on talking.

Chapter VII

Help from a Prayer

It may sound appealing to talk about accepting Jesus as the Christ and to claim that we can live his authority in our lives, but, as we have just indicated, Jesus is more than talk, and we must do more than talk about him and make claims for him.

Are we able to live with him? Is there a way we can be helped to achieve that goal? We may be prepared to admit that Jesus' resurrection from the dead and bestowal of the Spirit are marks of his glory, and that his presence with us now in the Spirit initiates his second coming, but a difficulty remains insofar as his glory and his presence are discernible only to faith. It would be easier if we were overwhelmed by him; that is the kind of coming of the Messiah the early Jews expected, and it is the kind of coming of the Christ most Christians want. We may not like the arrangement the way it is, but the fact that faith is necessary for the discernment of Christ's presence and glory is something we must accept in the mystery of God. Even so, we should remember that the necessity of discerning Christ's presence and glory by faith does not keep Christ from being real and independent of our faith.

Actually, the situation may not be as unusual as we think. Most of what we take to be the obvious aspects of the world in which we live, the features of the world which crowd in upon us and about which we seldom think, need special agents to be recognized; our eyes alone see color, our ears alone detect sound, while only the taste buds on our tongue detect flavors. The tongue does not see, and the eyes do not hear. More significant, perhaps, is the fact that love alone allows us to recognize the needs of others, and only the trust of others allows us fully to know ourselves.

Different things are discovered in different ways, and since, as we have noted, religious faith is a special kind of openness to God, it is not unreasonable for God to reveal himself in a special way to those who are prepared to receive him. Granting the radical difference between us, God and we are persons, and persons can reveal themselves to each other only where certain personal conditions exist. I do not reveal my inmost thoughts to someone who is hostile to me, nor do I expose my needs to someone I do not trust. The openness of love and trust are necessary if friends are to know each other for the persons they most deeply are. The more personal and intimate the communication, the more open persons must be to each other. Could anything require more trusting openness—more faith—than the intimate knowledge of God's life and love he offers to share with us in Jesus, his Son?

Friendship is an intimate relationship. It takes years to develop a close friendship, and growth in such friendship never ceases, as true lovers are aware. Love knows no end, for it is an on-going life of mutual sharing. When Jesus told his disciples, "I have called you friends, for all that I have heard from my Father I have made known to you" (Jn. 15:15), he indicated that what his openness to the Father had enabled him to know of the Father, the disciples' openness to him had enabled him to share with them. Henceforth Jesus' openness to the Father was the disciples' openness; as friends of Jesus, the disciples were friends of God. What we know as Jesus' public life was actually the secret life of God revealed to us. Jesus' death on the cross is God's intimate love for us, as is Jesus' resurrection from the dead; if we remember that, it will not seem strange that faith, the openness to God we have been talking about, is necessary to know the crucifixion and resurrection for what they truly are. Because God is personal, intimacy with him occurs only under personal conditions, just as such intimacy occurs with us. Faith is not a formal object we either have or do not have; it is the door to intimacy with God.

In speaking of faith we have continued to speak of it in terms of openness, but, it may be remembered, we also described prayer as openness to God. We usually think of prayer as an expression of faith, one expression out of many, but there is a sense in which prayer is co-extensive with faith. If the co-extensiveness of faith and prayer were more widely recognized, prayer would be easier for many people than it presently is. Too often prayer is thought of as a highly specialized activity which is begun and ended in an highly formalized manner, and which, because of its special nature, produces highly specialized results which can be checked for in our prayer lives.

In prayer there are methods to follow, ladders to climb, plateaus to reach. We are told there are special difficulties along the way, and people of prayer often seem to be different than we are.

The most important thing about the prayer life is the *life,* not the prayer. Prayers are the words we use only in a secondary sense, and the highest types of prayer, because they are expressions of the deepest love, do not use words at all. Words would be a distraction. Love itself is a speaking.

The type of life we lead determines the type of prayer we can offer much more effectively than the type of prayer we offer determines the type of life we lead. To be sure our prayers influence our lives, but it is too easy to let beautiful words offer us a consolation other people discern as hypocrisy. Jesus himself called attention to that fact when he quoted Isaiah's prophecy, "This people honors me with their lips, but their heart is far from me. . . ." (Mk. 7:6; Mt. 15:8).

We are able to pray only to the extent that we are open to God, and whenever we are open to God we are praying. If we realized that, prayer would be easier for us, and the difficulties we have in prayer would not be special difficulties; they would be the difficulties we are familiar with in our daily lives. That does not make the difficulties any less difficult to overcome, but it does cut our difficulties in half! Prayer does not face us with any new difficulties. So often people with difficulties in their lives turn to prayer only to encounter a new set of difficulties. Their spiritual lives consist in the swapping of one set of problems for another. In addition to that, when things are going well in their spiritual lives, because those lives are separated from their lives in the world, they get no help in their daily lives from their prayers. They only feel the loss of not being able to hold one thought or one mood all day long. They know only broken resolves. The first traffic light shatters their spiritual peace of glass.

When our prayer lives are seen to be our daily lives, then our prayers are seen to influence our lives in an obvious manner. We live only one life with God, and that life is meant to be our prayer life. "Prayer is life" may be a better way of putting it than "Life is prayer," although both are true. "Faith is prayer" and "Prayer is faith" are also true, and that recognition furnishes an occasion to return to a discussion of how prayer can help us live our openness to Jesus as the Messiah.

In faith we open ourselves to Jesus and to God, and prayer is another way of describing such openness. Because it is to God that we open ourselves in prayer, and because he is with us and we are with him, we must be aware of God's speaking to us in our prayers, as well as of our speaking to God. What God says to us is more important than what we say to him, and God's message is always found in Jesus the Christ, God's last Word to us.

Just as faith is necessary in Jesus' presence and for his presence, so is prayer. Prayer can be a special aid in helping us realize God's presence—if it is the right kind of prayer. To be "right" the prayer must help us realize the presence of God in Jesus, keep before us who Jesus is, make us know ourselves only in Jesus, and prevent us from being satisfied with the prayer alone. Such a prayer would help us recognize the presence of Jesus as the Messiah, but does such a prayer exist?

We believe there is such a prayer and that it is called the Jesus Prayer. There may, in fact, be many prayers which would serve the purpose of which we are speaking, but for the reasons we will offer, we will consider only the one prayer we have mentioned.

The first reason for our concentrating on the Jesus Prayer is that it has been used by countless numbers of people, especially in the Eastern Church, for centuries. The Prayer is not original or exclusive. Thus its use puts us as individuals firmly within the community of faith called together by God's Word, within which alone God's covenant of salvation is found. So frequently, in trying to be intimate with God, we act as if we expect God to begin his concern for humankind with us, and as if he has said little if anything of significance to other people before our time.

We are frequently tempted to treat God's presence in past history as if God were not there at all. On such a view, history is only the record of dead people's approach to God. But if we think about God merely as other people tried to approach him in their lives, we set the terms: we look history over from our point of view and decide what was right and wrong in it. It and the people who lived before us are completely subject to our judgment. We let them speak before us (after all, they lived first), but we do not let them speak to us—or better, we do not let God speak through them to us. They speak their lines to each other; we observe the exchange and determine whether or not the conversation was worthwhile.

We must remember that Christianity began and continues because of God's initiative. God is in human lives because he moves first; the way he works in history and the way people have discovered him in their lives before our time are facts which help measure present-day Christians, not dead traces from the past we can discard to our benefit. The Bible is the norm of the Christian experience of God precisely because of God's presence to chosen people for his reasons, not ours.

By using the Jesus Prayer as the cornerstone of our relationship with God, we admit that God is more than his effect on us, and we confess that he came and started something *he* wanted in the world independently of us. That being the case, we have to listen to him as he speaks through others to us, instead of acting as if he has spoken for the first time in history to us.

A second reason for our concentrating on the Jesus Prayer is its relation to the biblical revelation. The Prayer itself is not biblical, but its orientation is. "Repent, believe, and be saved" is the Gospel formula. Jesus preached repentance as the only means of entering the kingdom of God, and although our modern highways should provide a better route to the kingdom than that, taking the route advised by others is a way we can let them speak to us in their own right. We even let God speak to us through them.

A third helpful feature of the Prayer also arises from its use by so many people for so long a time. God is different from us. We need his difference, but we find it difficult to let him into our lives. The Jesus Prayer, because of its use by others, has in itself the otherness of someone coming to us to say something to us. Thus our use of the Prayer is an escape from ourselves, the very thing the difference of God brings into our lives.

Chapter VIII

The Jesus Prayer

The form of the Jesus Prayer we shall consider is the form most used today:

> Lord Jesus Christ, Son of God,
> Have mercy on me, a sinner.

The Prayer is used in time with one's breathing, saying the first half of the first line on the inhale and the second half of the first line on the exhale; the same pattern is followed in the second line. When saying the Prayer, the meaning of the words, not the words themselves, should be concentrated upon, for, in traditional terminology, the Prayer is to be a "prayer of the heart," a prayer uttered with our whole being, not just with our lips. The Prayer is an attitude too immediate to be expressed in words, rather than a prayer we can say or look at in words.

Correlating the Prayer with one's breathing is often a difficulty for those first beginning the Prayer's use. The practice may suggest a mechanical approach to God which is distasteful. That feeling will ebb and flow as experience with the Prayer continues, but eventually the use of the Prayer in time with one's breathing will become quite natural.

Traditional advice advocates regularizing one's breathing for a while before beginning the Prayer. Breathing exercises have even been prescribed. There is nothing wrong with proceeding that way, and centuries of use back up such a method, but since prayer is an opening of oneself to God, fewer problems are presented to many people if they consciously open themselves to God and let his presence govern everything in them—including their breathing—rather than trying to work through their breathing to him. The association of breathing with prayer is habit-forming, however, and provides a ready occasion for prayer throughout the day.

The most important thing to stress is that the Prayer is being said to Jesus as the Christ, the Messiah, in the End Time he makes available to us. The Prayer is a way to practice the presence of God, but it is not a method for bringing God into our time. He came into our time to bring his time. We cannot do what he has already done; that is why, even with the utmost effort, we cannot make him present to us. We can, however, recognize his presence, and that is what the Jesus Prayer helps us do.

That the Prayer is said in the End Time is not stressed in the traditional instructions on the Prayer's use, but because the Prayer addresses and describes Jesus, and because Jesus is the Messiah, our use of the

Prayer helps us understand how we should live with the Messiah in the special time which is his.

The Jesus Prayer is addressed to the "Lord Jesus Christ, Son of God." We have already had a good deal to say about Jesus as the Christ, and we have occasionally referred to Jesus as Lord and Son of God. Let us now look more closely at the meaning of the last two titles. When we say "Son of God" in the Prayer we are doing something amazing, for we are referring to the power of the resurrection by a personal title instead of by a general description. Jesus is declared "Son of God" in power by the resurrection. As Paul said, Jesus was "designated Son of God in power according to the Spirit of holiness by his resurrection from the dead" (Rom. 1:4).

To be able to call Jesus "Son of God" as a Christian does *is* to experience the power of the resurrection. "Son of God" is exciting to say when it is fully meant. "Son of God" is a declaration, a recognition, a proclamation; it is participation in an event, not the mention of a past term for a dead person. It is the making of a claim based on our own experience.

No term is more disputed and problematic for biblical scholars than "Son of God." The meaning of the term has been disputed from Jesus' day to our own, but the very dispute brings a sense of peace and relaxation to the term's use in prayer. Calling Jesus "Son of God" is relaxing in the sense of "fulfilling" and "completing"; the term is a sabbath among the titles of Jesus. All other titles aim at it and find their fulfillment in it. To use the title in prayer and accept it in one's heart is to accept a claim achieved instead of wondered about. As the phrase is used in the Jesus

Prayer, it is said when one is exhaling, and thus its meaning is carried throughout the body in a feeling of release. It is a help to make a prolonged pause at this point in the Prayer, allowing the meaning of the title to sink into our being and hold us in its presence. It is a moment of peace, a recognition which fulfills our lives and assures us of the help we need when we go on to ask for mercy. It takes faith, as it takes breath in the Prayer, to call Jesus "Lord," but, having done so, we are rewarded with the effortless presence of the Son of God—just as the effortless release of exhaling follows our inhaling.

To say that Jesus is Lord with the recognition that he is Son of God is to remove him from a sliding scale with other human beings. Jesus as Lord is different from us; as Lord he is Absolute for us in the same way that God is Absolute and without rival. It is because Jesus as Lord is so different from us, while still living as we do in the world, that we can recognize his lordship only in the Holy Spirit; the recognition required is of such an unusual nature that we are not capable of it by ourselves alone. Our dependence on God is complete even in recognizing Jesus. Nothing in our salvation comes from us. God's love does it all. Again St. Paul goes to the heart of the matter when he states: "No one can say 'Jesus is Lord' except by the Holy Spirit" (1 Cor. 12:3).

To recognize Jesus as Lord is to recognize him, from within, as somehow a world in himself, as unique rather than inclusive, as omnipresent in his Spirit, as the Way, as the Truth, as the Life, as Savior, as the mystery of God come to us.

But if Jesus is so different, how do we know him?

How do we meet him? Through the testimony of others. There is no other way. We come to know Christ through those who know him. No one starts from scratch or meets Jesus in a vacuum. We meet him through his friends in whom he lives. If there are no such people, he cannot be met—and he would not be worth meeting. We meet Jesus as we meet other people, through introductions. Read with understanding, the Bible is such an introduction.

A trenchant critic of our time has said that the slavery of today is alienation. We are alienated from ourselves, which means we are lost to ourselves. To be redeemed we need to be found, to be loved, to be freed from our false selves so we can become our true selves. The recovery of ourselves is the redemption for which we long, and our alienation from ourselves is the slavery of which we ourselves are the masters. To be redeemed we must be chosen by someone else for our real selves. In Jesus we are chosen by God and loved by him, even while we are in our sin; that is the love shown in the crucifixion. Only God's love chooses us for our true selves in spite of ourselves, and by choosing us God enables us to become different than we are. In Jesus' resurrection God's love is shown to be even more powerful than the death we know is ours alone. Because Jesus is uniquely the love of God come to us, we have absolutely no alternative to him. He is our Lord; he is our Savior.

The Gospel according to Luke puts the insight in narrative form. After Jesus healed the demoniac in the land of the Gerasenes, Jesus told the man to return home and declare how much God had done for him. We read that the man "went away, proclaiming throughout the whole city how much *Jesus* had done for him" (Lk. 8:39, italics added). The demoniac did not know God apart from Jesus or Jesus apart from God. He recognized God's Son in the world and his life was changed. Our lives can be changed, too, by living with Jesus as the Son of God in the openness of the Jesus Prayer.

Chapter IX

Only in
Jesus' Presence

If people are surprised to learn that this is the End Time, they are equally surprised to learn what life in the End Time should be like. The manner in which we are called to live the victory of Jesus in the world is not the manner of life many people imagine for the second coming, but the appropriate way of acknowledging the presence of the Christ in our lives can be found in the Jesus Prayer. There, instead of rejoicing that our passive purity has been rewarded and that, as God's favored ones, we escape punishment, we ask for freedom from sin through the mercy of God. In the End Time, the defeat of death is seen to be the universalization of the cross, and the meaning of life is found in serving others in Jesus' name.

The manner in which we pray the last half of the Jesus Prayer indicates whether or not we are disciples of the Way addressed in the first half of the Prayer, and an attempt to draw out the implication of the last half of the Prayer will occupy the rest of our attention.

We should first observe that the use of the Prayer requires an admission from us about ourselves which is very different from the way we usually think of ourselves. In the Prayer, we find our very identity in our sin and we regard ourselves as basically sinners, for in the Prayer we approach Jesus only as sinners asking for mercy. Such an admission is distasteful to us.

We all know there have been times when we have sinned in the past, but those were the moments in which we have been taught to think of ourselves as having been less than ourselves. We may be sorry there were times we were not ourselves, but such lapses are what we should repent of and be sorry for. Use of the Jesus Prayer does not allow us the luxury of regarding ourselves as only occasional sinners.

There is a new fullness of reality accepted when we admit we are first of all sinners, a fullness which cannot be attained any other way. We recognize and accept the negativity of our lives with a new thoroughness, for we acknowledge the negativity we initiate as well as receive; we recognize our responsibilities and shortcomings, not just those of others. To call ourselves first of all sinners is to recognize and accept our whole lives as we live them. The recognition puts an end to pretending that our positive thoughts are all of us. It ends our pretense to being the all-sufficient engineers, the ones whose goals, purposes, and intentions are sufficient for everyone.

Sin requires a relation to another in order to be itself. We sin against others and we can sin against ourselves only if we belong to Another or think of ourselves as other than we actually are. Consequently, the recognition of ourselves as sinners opens us to others and forces us to admit a relation to them at a level we do not like to admit in our consciousness. It puts us in our place, a place with others, instead of allowing us to pretend we are sources of universal good. Even when we admit the good we intend comes from Another, if we only deal with our intentions for others, we ignore our actual relations with them. To admit we are sinners keeps us from trying to live a fantasy. We allow ourselves to be our whole selves, the selves we do not want to recognize as well as the partial selves we want to pretend we are.

When we recognize about ourselves what we don't want to, our smallness and meanness, we find that our relations to others change, for the way we relate to others—what we do to them, even if it is no more than ignoring them—is an aspect of ourselves that we can only learn from them. A person is not non-existent because we ignore him; he has something to say to us even if we pretend he is not there. We think we ignore people because of our power and sufficiency. We can *afford* to ignore them just as we can afford to spend money, we think to ourselves. Actually, we ignore them because of our poverty. We would rather appear rude than weak; we cannot manage them at the moment, so we pretend not to recognize them.

Our relations to others destroy our pretensions to self-sufficiency. I, for example, find it hard to receive something from other people in a way which acknowledges my dependence on them. I like to think of myself as making my way on my own resources; I am responsible for my stand and I prove my point. Working on a paper in college once, I wondered whether or not to refer to someone else who stated an insight before I did. I consulted a professor about the matter and was given the consoling advice that, if the words I used were mine, the truth belonged to no one. I did not have to acknowledge the other person. As far as abstract truth is concerned, it is only accidental if you, not I, discover it, but as we live our lives in relation to each other, accidental dependence can be total dependence. That you accidentally happened to be where I was drowning does not mean that I only accidentally depend on you for saving my life. If I get a new insight from a book I would not have read if you had not recommended it to me, can I abstract my dependence on you from the result of the insight in my life? As I think my thoughts, you need not be mentioned, for the thoughts after all are mine, not yours, but my life would have been different if it were not for you. So my life would be different if it were not for Jesus. My thoughts about him do not save me. He does.

Opening ourselves to our full relations to others opens us to Jesus in a new way. We receive him a new way and recognize him in a new way. He enters our lives doing something for us we cannot do for ourselves. It is no longer we who try to use him in God's name, but he who brings God's difference to us.

Since Jesus forgives our sins, we cannot possibly use a method, something we control, in our approach to him. In fact, we sin only to the extent that we are in control, only to the extent that our methods are used. He is the Messiah. He breaks forms and formulas; he fills our lives and breaks them with his newness rather than serving us in our old desires. As Servant, he saves us instead of obeying us; as servants we are freed by obeying him.

We cannot think ourselves into Jesus' presence, for we cannot think ourselves into being forgiven. We must accept forgiveness just as we must accept personal presence. Jesus' presence is forgiveness; to accept one is to accept the other, and neither is present without the other. To deny our need for forgiveness is to make his presence impossible. That is the unanimous witness of Christians who have gone before us. It is foolishness to human beings, but evidently it is the wisdom of God. At least that is the best testimony we have from those whose lives have been changed in Christ.

While most of us can, on occasion, admit that we are sinners, we also believe that the admission of sin, as sin itself, is something to get beyond. In fact, we believe that the acknowledgment of sin *is* the getting beyond it.

That is our mistake.

Acknowledging sin is the way we recognize Jesus, for it is only in Jesus' presence that we can know sin for what it is, and it is only in him that we get beyond sin. We must be in him to recognize sin, and only in him can we not sin. He is the Other against whom we sin and the Other who saves us from sin. Since it is ultimately he against whom we sin, only he can save us from it.

Our error is to think we can recognize sin by ourselves; if we could, then our recognition of it would be our passing beyond it. The truth of the matter is that if we could recognize all of our sin by ourselves, the recognition would destroy us. We cannot recognize all of our sin by ourselves. We need the presence of Jesus to be able to know our true selves, and we need his presence to save us from ourselves.

So much talk about sin may sound like the loss of maturity to contemporary ears. In the common witness of the Christian saints, however, such self-understanding is the maturity in Christ spoken of by Paul. The only dare we must take to discover the truth about ourselves is to let Jesus into the fullness of our lives. If Christianity is true because something happened, we can check Christianity's truth only by letting it happen to us for what it was claimed to be by those who knew it first, rather than by trying to correct their description from our point of view. If, excited by the witness of others and the peace they knew in their lives, we want what they experienced, we will never get it by denying their experience. But that is exactly what we do when we try to approach Jesus as anything but sinners.

Few things are lamented more in the Christian churches today than their lack of evangelical zeal. Church members know something is wrong, and they generally think, if the various polls we read in the papers are correct, that evangelism is the answer. We need to evangelize the world; we need to bring people back to the church; we need to fill our mortgage-bound buildings with new believers, the shrinking numbers of people in the pews lament. I have heard meetings and conferences call for evangelism again and again, and I have sat in meeting after meeting in which the techniques of evangelism are discussed. Over and over I hear people talk about how to spread the good news—the latest advertising and communication techniques are described—but the cost of employing those techniques frequently seems to condemn present-day evangelism to failure. The possibility of raising more money is one of the benefits of evangelism, and yet, because of our lack of evangelism, we do not have the money to be evangelistic. We are in a lose-lose situation.

General programming is necessary in the church, but, if the biblical witness is fundamental for us, we had better make sure we know what the good news is before we try presenting it to others. It is something of an embarrassment to many of the established churches which have supported biblical criticism and historical research that the more naive, literalistic, and unsophisticated denominations have a missionary zeal and fervor which is the envy of those who presumably know so much more about Christianity. Obviously, something genuine has been lost by some and found by others.

Acquaintance with Jesus as a person empowers those who are the most enthusiastic witnesses in the world. The good news does not cost money; in fact, the good news was bad news to at least one person with money to whom Jesus talked. But after the rich young man went away sorrowful because he had been told to sell what he had and give to the poor, Jesus went on to say that even the rich could be saved, for nothing is impossible with God (Mk. 10:17ff).

Money cannot buy the good news—that is part of

the good news! But the good news must be spread. Evangelism is witness. If a witness has had nothing happen to him, obviously his testimony will sputter and stammer. We can learn again from an incident in our Lord's life we quoted in the last chapter from the Gospel of Luke; this time we will quote from Mark. After Jesus had cured the demoniac in the land of the Gerasenes, he said, " 'Go home to your friends, and tell them how much the Lord has done for you, and how he has had mercy on you.' And he went away and began to proclaim in the Decapolis how much Jesus had done for him; and all men marveled" (Mk. 5:19f).

The demoniac knew the mercy of God because something had happened to him. Jesus said only that the man should go and tell others, but we read that he not only told but he also proclaimed to others how much Jesus had done for him. Can it be that although we sometimes talk about religion to others, we find it difficult to proclaim Jesus because we have no experience of anything he has done for us? We pray for his mercy, but we never seem to experience it. Can that be because we do not recognize his mercy where it is given? If his mercy is shown primarily in forgiving our sins, and we do not recognize that we are sinners, we will miss his mercy for obvious reasons.

We best recognize injustices, things we do not have and should, rather than what we should not have but do. We continue to look at God through our eyes instead of seeing ourselves in the eyes of Jesus. We refuse the mind of Christ (1 Cor. 2:16). We must know ourselves in the Spirit, that is, in the gift of God. It takes God's gift to recognize God's gift; it takes the gift of God's Spirit to recognize God's gift of his Son. Once we recognize God's gifts for what they are, all the world will know about them, for we will find it impossible to remain silent. Proclamation is more than talk; it is witness.

Chapter X

Awareness of Our Acceptance

One of the astonishing experiences of the Christian life is to find comfort in saying, "I am first of all a sinner." What foolishness from the point of view of the world! But the statement made by a Christian is a way of saying, "Jesus, you are first in my life."

We can fully acknowledge our sin only in Jesus' presence, and, looking at ourselves in his presence, we see ourselves defenseless, as we truly are, for the first time. We need forgiveness only in the presence of another, and we can get forgiveness only from another. That is why it would never occur to us to accuse ourselves of being first of all sinners when we are alone. Only in Jesus' company can we know ourselves, for as Christians we are first ourselves in him.

The biblical experience, as described, for example, in the Epistle to the Ephesians, speaks of this realization in Christ: "But God, who is rich in mercy, out of the great love with which he loved us, even when we

were dead through our trespasses, made us alive together with Christ (by grace you have been saved),
and raised us up with him, and made us sit with him
in the heavenly places in Christ Jesus, that in the coming ages he might show the immeasurable riches of his
grace in kindness toward us in Christ Jesus. For by
grace you have been saved through faith; and this is
not your own doing; it is the gift of God—not because
of works, lest any man should boast. For we are his
workmanship, created in Christ Jesus for good works,
which God prepared beforehand, that we should walk
in them" (Eph. 2:4–10).

It will pay us to look more closely at these words.
The passage describes the richness of God's mercy; his
richness is surely first known to us in his mercy, the
way he freely relates to us in Jesus. God's mercy is the
manifestation of his love. Existing by ourselves in our
sin we are actually dead, cut off from the life of God.
From the death which is the isolation we impose on
ourselves by sin, God in his love offers us life in
Christ. The translation says we are made "alive together with Christ," and we must grasp the full
strength of that statement. There is no preposition in
the Greek text: the idea of "together with" is expressed as part of the verb itself. We are alive only to
the extent that we live with Christ; we are dead without him and know life only in him. For Christians life
is a relation with God. That is why, by ourselves, we
are dead.

Living in the Christ we live in a new time; we are
saved from our old existence, which was actually a
death when compared to the life we have in him. Because life in Christ is offered to us as a gift, it is an of-

fering of grace; for us, then, our very life means to be saved by Jesus through the love of God.

The life we know in Christ is a participation in the life of resurrection, the life of heavenly permanence. Because there is but one Christ and he lives but one life, the only life we can know in him is the life of his victory already achieved. In him we are meant to reign over the problems of the world, not avoiding such problems but attacking them for what they are with the assurance that the strength with which we confront them is ultimately more powerful than they are. We are people of hope.

A second time in the text, within the compass of a few words, we are reminded that we have been saved from ourselves not by our own efforts but by the free gift of God. We cannot boast; we can only receive. Indeed, we receive so much from God in Christ (our dependence on Jesus for life is total, for without him we are dead) that our life in Christ is nothing less than our new creation. "Creation" means "total dependence." Since we know God's life, true life, only in Jesus, our being brought to life in him is our being recreated by him. We are reborn, for we are brought forth with a total newness. Created in Jesus, God uses us as agents through whom his newness is extended to the whole world in the End Time, ultimately to incorporate everything which exists into the redemption he offers. We are his work and as his work we work, walking surely with him in the way he has prepared for us, the way of love and self-giving.

It is because saying of ourselves, "I am first a sinner," means, "I am first myself with Jesus," that we do not want to get beyond the admission of our sin. We do not need to get beyond it! The recognition of sin is the recognition of Jesus, and if one is first with Jesus, nothing more is possible. That realization can bring us to a new understanding of the familiar words, "I am the Alpha and the Omega, the first and the last, the beginning and the end" (Rev. 22:13). The right beginning *is* the end; Jesus the Alpha *is* the Omega; once with him there is no place else to go. We can rejoice always.

The Jesus Prayer seems to begin with a conclusion—the condemnation of ourselves because of our sin—but it ends with a beginning of freedom and joy.

We have got to learn that we become strong by being freed, instead of thinking we can be freed by our strength. To admit we are sinners all day long, with every breath, we must be in the presence of God, as we have indicated, for only with God is the admission possible. But if the Prayer is used with constancy it is not morose or morbid. When the Prayer becomes non-verbal and is no longer just a sentence composed of words, it is a way of having ourselves in perspective; it is the open door to gratitude and thankfulness. Properly used, the Prayer is actually the awareness of our acceptance by Jesus, the awareness of our acceptance in the love of the Father. To call ourselves sinners in the Prayer is never a badge of courage, something of which to be proud; instead the Prayer is the realization that what is happening is real, that God is accepting us as persons, that we are not trying to talk ourselves into something by ourselves. Opening ourselves in the Prayer precludes any possibility of our trying to take care of ourselves by ourselves; thus we are freed from ourselves. The Prayer separates us from the selves we produce when we pretend to look outward while we are really looking inward. Such activity is a trick we frequently play on ourselves. We become more self-conscious when we heighten our conscious effort to forget ourselves, and we become more anxious when we anxiously try to avoid anxiety. The Prayer cuts the wordiness of religion with a confrontation which devours evasiveness.

Another benefit which can be ours through use of the Prayer is a new-found ease of being with other people. When we fully accept ourselves as sinners, we will find it easy to be with others on any occasion. We will then not find ourselves so precious that it is an effort to pay attention to them, nor will we have to pretend they are important to keep up appearances. Other people are important just because they are there and we can be with them. How different that experience is than secretly having to decide within ourselves, while we are standing face to face with someone, whether or not we want really to let him or her into our lives. The realization of ourselves produced by the Prayer freely allows us to go different places, instead of pretending to be in different places, while we never leave ourselves. Enjoyment becomes possible. So does rejoicing; innocence becomes a perfection to progress toward rather than a childishness to grow out of. Relaxation becomes a condition of our lives instead of a goal. We are seldom aware how much of our energy goes toward protecting ourselves instead of toward being ourselves; in fact, many of us mistake protecting ourselves for being ourselves, for we spend all of our lives in our defense and know nothing else.

Living the Jesus Prayer, we are not afraid, and we

do not anticipate what will happen to us. We receive ourselves from God; he guards us and that guarding is our peace." Then the peace of God which is beyond our utmost understanding, will keep guard over your hearts and your thoughts, in Christ Jesus" (Phil. 4:7 NEB). But the best part about living the Prayer is that we do not have to keep telling ourselves not to be afraid and finding our words unconvincing just because we have to keep saying them. Telling ourselves to be at peace is not the same thing as being peaceful, and the necessity to keep telling ourselves to be calm is found only where peace is lacking: the saying emphasizes the absence instead of supplying the need. A religion of words is a religion of despair and disappointment.

Who would think that the blossom of Christian joy grows from the seed of admitting we are first of all sinners? But it does.

To ask Jesus, the Messiah, for mercy in the End Time does not leave us with the feeling of self-accusation; instead, we are flooded with the feeling of acceptance, the acceptance of our real selves by Jesus—the selves we do not have to pretend to ourselves about. The prayer for mercy is drawn beyond itself by God's love into a constant rejoicing at the extent of his mercy. God's mercy is not a forgetting, a wiping clean, an erasure. It is more positive than that. His mercy is new life in the Christ, an experience of the power of the resurrection expressed as freedom in the world.

To ask Jesus for mercy is to be judged by the resurrection rather than trying to grasp the resurrection for ourselves; such judging is how we receive the power of the resurrection as God's gift. Only in Jesus can we know our sin, but it is Jesus who said, "I am the resurrection and the life" (Jn. 11:25). Only if we know the resurrection as a gift can we know the resurrection at all. Death is the total absence of human power. To admit our total dependence on God before we physically die is the way to receive before death the gift which overcomes death.

Calling on Jesus with the faith of the Jesus Prayer, life becomes a privilege; life itself becomes the gift of mercy. Life is comfort, a wellspring of blessing. It is good to be alive! Jesus is life. Thanksgiving is natural, for one has been forgiven. Alleluia!

We pray,

Lord Jesus Christ, Son of God,
Have mercy on me a sinner,

knowing that the crucifixion is our acceptance and the resurrection is God's mercy!

Chapter XI

Death and Sin

Talking with a friend one day, he confided that if he were listing concerns which had persisted and bothered him throughout his life, death and sin would be near the top of the list. Death, he said, had always bothered him in a more spontaneous, and in that sense more natural, way than sin; and he went on to add that, if the truth were known, one of the things which bothered him most about sin was that it most often did not bother him enough. I knew what he meant.

The fear of death has been more immediate and real to me also than the fear of sin. I anticipate death with a fear much stronger than I anticipate sin. The Christian Gospel has always made the closest association between death and sin; the two have, in fact, been identified with each other, but in my life the identity has been something I have heard from others rather than something I have experienced myself.

As the years have gone by, the presence of death

has become more real to me. Perhaps that is because I am now entering the time of life known as "post middle-age." When I was younger and for one reason or another had a sudden fear of death, I was quickly able to quiet myself by remembering that—on the average—I was too young to die. Now death is an horizon within which more and more of life appears. But as I get closer to death with each passing day, a strange thing seems to be happening: as my death gets closer, I can honestly say that I am beginning to fear it less.

At the time I am beginning to fear death less, however, I also find that I am beginning to fear sin more. In what has been a significant discovery for me, I believe that my lessening fear of death is actually the result of my increasing fear of sin. I am beginning to discover that sin *is* death. Once that discovery has been made and we realize that Jesus saves us from our sin, we can face death with a new assurance that Jesus saves us from that too. The End Time is our door to the future.

A fear of death is natural, and we want to overcome it. Our fear of sin is not so natural, for it has become our nature to sin. Death is real for us because we know it will affect our whole being; sin is not so real because it too frequently seems to be no more than a matter of words.

The biblical account of death says that death is the result of sin. Sin released death as we know it into the world, but at this stage of the world, when sin has become so natural to us and we are unable even to recognize our sin by ourselves alone, death is a better means for helping us understand sin than sin is for helping us understand death. Let us then, in these Last

Days, take the New Testament proclamation of Jesus seriously and use the reality of our death as the key to understanding the reality of our sin.

Taking that lead, we are confronted with the fact that our sin exists in the same world that our death does. That is the world God enters in Jesus; all three—death, sin, Jesus—must be recognized with the same reality or we do not know any one of them. Our fear of death is real and must itself become our fear of sin, for if we think sin is less than death, we do not recognize how much sin affects our relation to God. The very strength of death's destruction is the strength of sin in our lives with God, and until Jesus' victory makes as much difference to our desire to sin as it does to our fear of death, we do not know his victory. Nor do we know our lives as they should be. We do not accept our real selves.

When we think about our death and about our sin, both our sin and our death remain in our perspective; we handle them and control them as extensions of our thought. Fear comes when we find ourselves in death's perspective instead of having it in ours. Then it comes to us instead of we to it, and we know the total fear of something outside our control which destroys us by its strangeness. If we let Jesus bring as much difference to us from beyond us as death threatens to do, then we can see how different we should be; then we can recognize how terrible our sin is for the first time, and then we can recognize how much God loves us to save us from death and sin, each in the other. Then we can accept our real selves. By knowing Jesus and willing what he wills, we become his friends, completely dependent upon him and confident in him, before physical death. Jesus with us as our friend in death is the means by which we overcome death.

The power with which we must accept ourselves is the power of death. By doing that we can be real with Jesus and know how real he is for us, for he has already laid down his life for us. "Greater love has no man than this, that a man lay down his life for his friends. You are my friends if you do what I command you" (Jn. 15:13f). Only by this means can we know his love, for it comes from outside us just as death does.

On the surface, death and sin do not seem to have much in common, but that is why we need to take seriously the deep and uncompromising witness of those who knew Jesus before us as a means of helping us get beneath the surface of things. We are meant to learn from the experience of others, for without their experience, we could not be Christians. Death happens to us; sin, on the other hand, is something we do. The two seem very different. What we need to discover is that the effect of the sin we do and the death we suffer are the same, even though the source of each appears to be different. Whenever we sin we try to kill whomever we sin against, even if we sin against ourselves. When we sin we cooperate with our opposite— with our death—even though "we are most ourselves" when sinning. Sin is our responsibility in its origin, but it is our enemy (death) in its effect. To see the oneness of sin and death is to be able to accept the wholeness of life as a Christian for the first time.

If a person is a Christian, he or she should be able to walk into a hospital room (one's own or someone else's), a nursery, a wedding, or a funeral with the same tranquility and hope.

How is that possible?

By viewing sin through the reality of death and accepting Jesus as our Savior precisely because we are saved from sin and death in him. The Christian is the person whose life is so real that his peace is not disturbed by looking at the world through the eyes of death. Christian joy is born only because of the passing-through of death. The manner in which a Christian is able to "see with the eyes of death" does not mean that a Christian tries to go through death to Jesus. To see with the eyes of death is not to think only one thought, "death," and it is not to paint all the flowers in the garden black. Jesus becomes our death because he is our Life. Wonder! *To know the joy of life with the certainty of death.*

Jesus consumes death, turning it into something else by using it, as we turn food into energy by eating it. That is how Jesus tasted death for everyone (Heb. 2:9). Consumed by Jesus, death's reality becomes the reality of his life. Jesus' death killed death, but each of the deaths must be as real as the other for them to affect each other. The *reality* of death's destruction is the only dimension of death that continues after Jesus' resurrection from the dead. The reality of death minus its destructiveness is all that is left of death in the risen Lord; death's reality is absorbed into the power of Jesus' life and is the sense in which we know death in knowing Jesus. We cannot know life without death or death without life in Jesus, but that fact does not make the Christian life morbid, just real.

For the Christian, to see things with the eyes of death is not to put patches over one's eyes. Life is not blocked out; only the superficial glare is gone. So to view life is a way for our religion to affect the world in which our bones are a part instead of the world of empty words alone. It is our bones which are laid in the grave. We need a Savior as real as they. We need a Savior who has had his bones laid in a grave but who can hear us now. To accept life in the death of Jesus is the way to enjoy life by not being caught up in what is less than life.

The joy of those who have been given a reprieve in this world, those who have had a critical illness and recovered, those who have looked death in the face but have escaped, is a distant approximation to the life we know in Christ. The "new life" experienced by people recovering from a critical illness is based on their confrontation with death. They find themselves strengthened with the latter's reality as they begin to re-enter the world of those who were not ill. They appreciate the small things in life that others take for granted and pay no attention to at all. We will never know peace until we can accept all of reality, even death, for what it is. In Christ we "see with the eyes of death," but that means that in Christ we have already passed through death. Jesus alone has passed through death to a more glorious life. The only victory we know is his, but he comes to share it with us as the Messiah.

Chapter XII

Accepting the Cross
as a Christian

In the Messiah's time, things are seen differently than they are in our time. In the different perspective of the End Time, the cross is known as the way God accepts us instead of condemning us. To be told to take up our cross and follow Jesus is not a way God taunts us by asking us to do something which revolts us. It is not a morbid goal God sets for us beyond us. Instead, Jesus' death on the cross is the way God enters our deepest lives in order to become intimate with us; it is the completeness of God's acceptance of us as we are, as nothing less than Jesus' crucifiers. The cross is the way God gives himself to us at our worst so that he alone can make us our best.

If we try to accept God at our best we are never freed from ourselves, for by our best we try to capture God. We try to save ourselves and, by so doing, we become incapable of a total acceptance of him. If part of us does not need God, that part of us is untouched by him when he comes.

We need God to save us from ourselves.

When we see the cross as God's way of saving us from ourselves, the "way of the cross" becomes the intimate way we become ourselves, rather than the way we are lost to ourselves. Then the cross, instead of calling us to submit to a source of external suffering, calls us to become our true selves at the expense of our false selves. Christ on the cross embraces us, and only in the completeness of that embrace can we embrace God as his new creatures. That is the sense in which the cross is the means of repentance—the means of changing our basic disposition toward life, which is what the biblical word "repentance" means in its roots.

God's call to repent is not a menacing threat of punishment and vengeance, intended to intimidate us by force; it is a call of comfort and mercy. To repent means to turn from ourselves to the God who is our true Comforter. He wants us to come to him so badly that he gave his Son for us on the cross. The cross is his self-giving out of love for us, not a threat he holds over us.

As most often seen, salvation through the cross is not attractive because it appears to be our condemnation instead of our acceptance. Easter redemption seems to be something standing behind the cross; it appears to be offered to us only after we are crucified, instead of being the redemption offered to us, the crucifiers, in the very act of our violence. The crucifixion is the proof that God loves us before we love him, for in the crucifixion God loves us even when we are most unlike him.

The power of the resurrection is the only means by which the cross of Jesus can be presented in its true nature. Only the resurrection gives the cross its Christian meaning. If we know the cross in the power of the resurrection, we can joyfully embrace it as the means of our salvation, for we can die to ourselves only to the degree we already live with God in the resurrected Jesus.

By God's alchemy the power of the resurrection becomes for us the power of repentance. The way we rejoice in God's love for us is by repenting of our sins so that we can live more completely in him. Our lives being filled with the dying to ourselves made possible by embracing God's saving power in the cross, the physical death we do not choose, but which comes to us anyhow, is no longer fearful. The death no one rightly chooses is thus redeemed by the death we can rightly choose, our death to sin. Death to our false selves is the only way to obtain the release of our true selves: the cross and resurrection of Jesus are the means by which we can become our true selves, for we are ourselves only in God's will for us.

The most horrible thing in the world—the cross as the instrument of Christ's death—becomes the most comforting thing in the world when we recognize its positive purpose in our lives. Then we can accept the cross as the means of our salvation instead of keeping it at a distance from us as the means of our destruction. Only when we freely identify with the cross within our lives can the power of the resurrection be experienced in those lives. Only by experiencing acceptance—and the most radical acceptance is that of Jesus on the cross—can we accept. Our total acceptance is necessary if we are to be totally accepting.

New life in Christ is a new creation. As such it can only be received; it can only be accepted. That means we cannot start our new lives by trying to appropriate the power of the resurrection in a positive way for ourselves, for that power is too much to be used by us. It releases us from ourselves for God's service instead of helping us attain our ideals, no matter how noble those ideals may be. We rise by God to God.

Only the person who has accepted Jesus on the cross and who knows he or she has been accepted by God in Jesus on the cross can know the power of the resurrection, for the power is *of* resurrection, i.e., of acceptance, not avoidance. Christ does not live because he avoided death but because his life was stronger than death.

To know the power of the resurrection we must first be able to accept that power. But acceptance is the meaning of the cross, for, as we have indicated, the cross is total acceptance. In accepting the Father's gift of the cross, we accept the power of the resurrection; no other act or wish is necessary. For us, it is not a matter of first dying to ourselves and then hoping for the power of the resurrection. Each—dying to self and resurrection—is the means of the other. Each is equally God's gift. It is when we think of the cross as our work and the resurrection as God's response to it that our God is no longer the God of love. Love only gives gifts, for love is gift; love can never be earned or deserved. Fully to accept the cross as gift is to begin a life of love with the God who is Love. Only by accepting the thoroughness of his love can we receive the glory of his Christ; in that sense, the cross is for us the key to the liberating glory of God.

The power of the resurrection is the love given on the cross!

Wonder . . .

Mystery.

Chapter XIII

"Glorious Liberty"

We have been attempting, since Chapter IX, to explore some of the implications of the use of the last half of the Jesus Prayer. We have suggested that just as people are surprised to hear that we now live in the End Time, so they are surprised to learn what life within the End Time should be like. Jesus is the Messiah, and the Spirit is, at one time, the glory of Jesus as the Christ and the means by which the true nature of Jesus is discovered. The Spirit is also the means by which Jesus is present with us after his resurrection and ascension in the beginning of his second coming.

The principal concern of all the Gospel accounts of the resurrection is to show that the very Jesus who walked the streets of Jerusalem and Galilee was the Jesus who rose from the dead and who now sits at the right hand of the Father (Eph. 1:20). Jesus is glorified by his resurrection and ascension, and by the outpouring of the Spirit, but his personal nature is not changed by those events. As the Book of Revelation puts it in the rich symbolism of its mystical vision, the Lamb which stands triumphantly before the throne of God stands "as though it had been slain" (Rev. 5:6). The Jesus who reigns, in other words, is precisely the Jesus who was crucified.

When we think of Jesus as the Messiah, we must remember that he is the same Jesus who so loved us that he hung on the cross for us. People are too often tempted to think of the Jesus who has promised to come again as a quite different Jesus from the one who lived as a servant of others and told his disciples to serve as he had served. Instead of finding the glory of God in service, people are tempted to think that the glory of God changes Jesus into an unrelenting Judge. It is as if God's glory makes Jesus a different person than he was while he lived in the world, instead of God's glory being found in Jesus' self-giving life in the world. Our concepts of glory seem always to be at odds with God's revelation.

It is because Jesus remains who he was, even after he is recognized to be the Messiah, that the Jesus Prayer can be the key to our lives with him as the Messiah. There were no doubt people using the Prayer in past centuries who were not fully aware of the implications of praying to Jesus as "Christ," but their experience of the presence of Jesus was genuine and says something important to us. Because Jesus is addressed as "Christ" in the Prayer, however, we understand that full recognition must be given to his nature as the Messiah. So we have tried to show what the consequences of Jesus' being the Christ are for our lives and for the world. It is our contention that we use the Jesus

Prayer in the End Time, but in the End Time it is the same Jesus who first lived on earth who is with us in the Spirit. That being the case, the Prayer teaches us that our complete dependence on Jesus for mercy does not change from his first coming to his second. Our present lack of recognition of such dependence, as a matter of fact, is what is holding up the consummation of the second coming!

In Jesus' second coming, we need to ask for his mercy as much as people needed to ask for it during his first coming. Only Jesus' presence with us enables us to discover what sinners we are, so the fact of his being with us in his second coming does not allow us to forget who we are and turn judgmentally toward others.

Still, life in the second coming does consist in a turning from ourselves toward others. The difference between the proper and improper turning toward others in the End Time is not so much in the turning as in what the turning is for. In the Spirit of the Christ, the turning toward others is for service, not condemnation. The turning is for acceptance, not judgment. People judge themselves in the light of Christ; they do not need us to judge them. The kingdom of God is a community, traditionally called the communion of saints, and it is that kingdom which entered the world in Jesus and which is presently in process of completion. As a communion, the kingdom grows by concern for others, not in isolation from them.

To turn toward others in acceptance is to turn toward them in service. That is the surprising freedom offered to us in the Messiah's coming; that is the life we shall now examine in more detail; and that is the life to which we had reference when we earlier said that, in the End Time, the cross is the key to the liberating glory of God. Jesus was raised from the dead by the glory of God (Rom. 6:4). God's glory is liberating, and in his glory, that is, in the Spirit, the freedom we know in the Messiah's name should be the sign that the End Time has come to the struggling world. As Paul tells us, "The creation waits with eager longing for the revealing of the sons of God; for the creation was subjected to futility, not of its own will but by the will of him who subjected it in hope; because the creation itself will be set free from its bondage to decay and obtain the glorious liberty of the children of God" (Rom. 8:19–21). The "glorious liberty of the children of God" belongs to those who recognize Jesus to be the Christ and who live in the kingdom he came to establish.

In the beginning of his Letter to the Colossians, Paul affirms that the kingdom the Messiah came to inaugurate has been established, for Paul, referring to action which has already been taken, says that God the Father "has delivered us from the dominion of darkness and transferred us to the kingdom of his beloved Son, in whom we have redemption, the forgiveness of sins" (Col. 1:13f).

Jesus redeems us by liberating us, for "to redeem" is "to liberate." The Christ is our deliverer, the one who sets us free by forgiving us our sins.

In the beginning of Luke's Gospel, after Jesus had been led by the Spirit into the wilderness and had returned in the power of the Spirit into Galilee, we are told that word about him spread throughout the region. Returning to Nazareth, he stood up to read in the synagogue and was given the book of the prophet Isaiah. He read, "The Spirit of the Lord is upon me, because he has anointed me to preach good news to the poor. He has sent me to proclaim release to the captives and recovering of sight to the blind, to set at liberty those who are oppressed. . . ." (Lk. 4:18).

Anointed by the Spirit of the mysterious God beyond all creation, Jesus is to bring good news to the poor and "to proclaim release for prisoners and recovery of sight for the blind; to let the broken victims go free," as the New English Bible translates the same passage. After Jesus closed the book he said, "Today this Scripture has been fulfilled in your hearing" (v. 21).

Jesus came to liberate those who without him had no hope, the people who were trapped, bound, and burdened in the world; he came to the sick, to the poor, to captives and sinners, to those held mechanically by forces beyond their control; he came to people controlled by other people, controlled by events and powers beyond them. He came to people who had no expectations of a better life; he came to those who had no future, only a present which was engulfed by the past, whose future could be predicted because it would be no different from the past. Jesus came to those whose lot seemed to be determined by fate; they were the people life pressed down upon and whose will was regarded no more than a high wind regards a candle.

But when Jesus came to such people unpredictable things began to happen. Their actual experience became different from predictions made by others about them. They were not molded by the past; instead they were liberated by a strange new power. That was the good news. The presence of Jesus was the unpredictable thing which happened to them. God came to them from beyond the world, so his presence was not predictable in terms of the world.

Jesus' presence with those who had no hope in their lives was the source of the new power in their lives. Predictions always abstract from actual conditions. They tell what will happen if certain conditions prevail. If conditions change, the necessity of a prediction's coming true is destroyed; we are liberated from the prediction's conclusion. If I stay out in the sun for hours, I will get a sunburn, but if I do not stay out that long, or if I cover myself with clothing or lotion, I will not be burned. What actually happens is determined by conditions outside of the prediction and over which the prediction has no control.

The presence of Jesus as the Christ with us is something new in our lives today, and when the new is present, something different occurs. We are freed from old predictions. Life in the End Time is marked by freedom, a freedom for which the whole creation has been waiting and which makes us the agents of God's re-creation of the world.

Chapter XIV

The Scandal of Freedom

We are set free in Christ, and, according to the words of Jesus himself reported in John's Gospel, "if the Son makes you free, you will be free indeed" (Jn. 8:36). Paul tells the Galatians that they were called to freedom, and he makes his claim the strongest way possible when he says, "For freedom Christ has set us free" (Gal. 5:1).

What does freedom mean in our lives? One kind of freedom comes from knowing another person. We live in a world of persons, and we need to be free in it.

Friends are liberating. Standing uncomfortably and self-consciously in a room full of strangers we feel released when we discover a friend in the crowd. We become ourselves. Not to know other people is a source of insecurity. What will they think? What will offend them? What will please them? God knows us, and in Christ he has called us friends. "You are my friends.... No longer do I call you servants...." (Jn.

15:14f). As we know him in Jesus, God enters our lives to set us free. Ultimate freedom in the world is to know that God is our friend.

Writing to the Romans, Paul says again that we have been set free in Christ. He details that claim by saying we have been set free from the law, sin, fear, and death. We know what fear and death are, but law and sin, in Paul's sense, are not so clear to us today.

For Paul, law and sin are intimately connected with fear and death. The meaning of all the terms Paul used can be summarized as our struggle to do things for ourselves. Put that way, what Paul wants deliverance from sounds like our goal. Self-sufficiency is what we want to develop as countries and as individuals. Growth in autonomy is a way of measuring maturity. We expect our children to grow up and do things for themselves. But the quest for self-sufficiency requires that we be self-centered, and the more self-centered we are the more we fear death—the loss of ourselves.

Struggling for ourselves we are bound up in ourselves. Think of self-centered people you know. Is there not a sameness, a repetition in their lives—and a boredom in yours when you have to be with them? No matter what you talk about or try to do with such people, they always project themselves as the primary center of interest.

Christian freedom is not the struggle for ourselves but release from ourselves. Instead of being bound up in ourselves we are available to other people and for other things. That is what freedom is all about; it brings openness, newness, variety, mobility, and release into our lives. Is not that how we want to live?

We are so frequently burdened by our anxiety and fear. We fear illness; we fear to stand up for what we believe; we wonder what our enemies will do to us; the constant change occurring in the world threatens us; large numbers of people find it hard to relax and go to sleep.

We must assert our freedom in the Messiah. He releases us from our burdens so that we can face our problems, secure in the power of God. The Church is not meant to be an immobile fortress with unchanging battlements used to defend the faithful against the attacks of the world; it is meant to be a moving army of the people of God on the attack in the world. The people of God are meant to march in the world, rejoicing on the way, shouting with the joy of freedom.

There are, indeed, people in the world who are alone, frightened, isolated, intimidated, fearful, forlorn, insecure, defensive, but they are not Christians. Christians are freed from such bondage. In Jesus, God is that wonderful face in the crowd, the one who says, "Come over here; I have been looking for you. I am your friend."

To be with someone we love is to be set free.

The presence of a person we love liberates us from everything else. His or her presence becomes our world, and in it we meet other people and the other events of life. To be with a loved one is to be unencumbered; it is to be fully where one is, available, open, loving. It is not to talk about such things; it is the living of them. The liberating presence of another person is not the goal of human activity; it is the basis for it.

Freedom in itself is openness to other things. It is

not being bound to any one thing. It is the ability to see; it is an unpainted canvas. Freedom seeks its content from the other, hungry for encounter. It is adventure and journey. Freedom cannot be itself by staying home and looking at itself.

Jesus offers us freedom because he is Lord of heaven and earth, the Christ. It is as Lord that Jesus rules the world, thereby setting us, his servants, free in the world. Christians claim that "his service is perfect freedom," but they go on to claim that freedom is service.

To mention service when one is extolling the advantages of freedom may seem to spoil the promise of Christian freedom to some who thought they might be interested in it. There appear to be strings attached to freedom in Christ. Does that fact contaminate it? Is the freedom free enough?

Paul, we have seen, puts the matter as strongly as he can when he says that "for freedom Christ has set us free" (Gal. 5:1). There is no limit there. Freedom is for freedom. That statement gets us to the true problem of Christian freedom: it is too free! It is too unlimited, and it is too immediate. It is too unlimited because it frees us from ourselves and our expectations; it is too immediate because it frees us before we are ready.

Christian freedom, like everything Christian, does not come in pieces. We either have it and use it or we do not. Freedom in Christ is not the obligation to become free from fear, anxiety, anger and other dangers which trouble us. It is freedom from the attempt to become free!

In Christ we are free from the expectations of

others, but, even more liberating, we are free from the expectations of ourselves. Jesus does not magically free us from our inabilities and limitations; instead he frees us from worry and embarrassment about them. He frees us from our pride, in other words. He frees us from needing to pretend to others for our sake.

Christian freedom is a marvelous and mysterious experience. It scandalizes—with the scandal of Jesus—the good sense of the world. Reason is outraged by it, but our lives are released.

True freedom in ourselves is from ourselves. Freedom is mobility. We do not need to express ourselves only one way. How frequently it is that a compulsive, insecure person is mistaken for a free person just because he or she has political or economic power at his or her disposal. A person who is driven to do just one thing and does it at the expense of others is not demonstrating freedom; such a person is exercising the dominance of his or her self-bondage over others. To be able to do only *this* now may mean that I have dominance over you, but it manifests a lack of freedom in me. If I am truly free, I am free not to offend others by my freedom. I am free to put myself last instead of first; I am free from myself instead of for myself.

Freedom is the ability to accept something when one does not have to. Such ability is power. Freedom enables us to enjoy the world, and such enablement is power. The offense—that is, the scandal—to reason of life in Christ is that a person living that life has been freed from all duty, right, "ought," and restraint. Such a person wants to do what he or she does and thus lives each moment in an unencumbered way. To talk about doing what we ought without feeling it a duty sounds like a paradox to reason, but it is victory when lived.

Freedom is nothing less than the loss of one's life. But it is a loss which is lived as gain. In that way the free person has already overcome death in the victory of Christ.

A free person is the master of time. Time becomes a means of living, not the end of living; freedom bursts time's restrictions, for no matter what we planned to do, we are available to what happens at the moment. A free person knows no interruptions.

The intimacy of Jesus' presence with us is the degree of our freedom. As the Christ, he liberates us and sets us free. He, the only one who is free—the only one who has overcome death, the ultimate bondage—is the only one who is able to bestow freedom. Since freedom can be gotten only from Jesus, to be free is to live in him.

As Christians, we know we are free only in Jesus, and yet we are afraid to let Jesus make the difference. Why?

To make the difference Jesus must really be here with us. His presence has consequences we are not prepared for if he is absent. We always feel more comfortable settling for the familiar. We are more comfortable with our problems than with Jesus' solution. His solution—he—brings something different to us. In him we are not ourselves anymore.

If Jesus is here, we can do things we could not do without him. Consequently, the only way we can show that he is with us is by doing things we could not do without him. We are afraid to let him be as real as we are. We are afraid to live the life of faith, and yet faith in him is the only way we can overcome fear. We must not try to be different. We have been liberated from that. We must let Jesus be different. We must let him be the Christ and let his difference show in us. We need Jesus if we are to live the freedom of God, for, without Jesus, God's freedom would make us too dizzy to stand. God's freedom is too absolute in itself alone; it is too much for us without Jesus for its content.

The freedom of God is of one kind only, the freedom found in the Son. Jesus is the means by which God's freedom becomes effective in the world. Jesus is the one to hang on to, the one reference never lost, when everything else changes. He is the stability which makes freedom possible: "Jesus Christ is the same yesterday and today and forever" (Heb. 13:8).

Chapter XV

Free To Serve

Paul tells the Galatians, "For you were called to freedom, brethren; only do not use your freedom as an opportunity for the flesh, but through love be servants of one another" (Gal. 5:13). To love another is to give oneself to another, that is, to serve the other. A person who uses power as "an opportunity for the flesh" is a slave to the flesh; to serve others in love is the life of the End Time made possible in the glory of the Spirit. Paul goes on in his Epistle to the Galatians to describe life in the Spirit as the life of freedom. He writes, "But if you are led by the Spirit you are not under the law" (Gal. 5:18). To be under the law is to be under restraint; it is to live under bondage. But the "fruit of the Spirit is love, joy, peace, patience, kindness, goodness, faithfulness, gentleness, self-control; against such there is no law" (Gal. 5:22f). There can be no law against the fruit of the Spirit, becasue it is impossible to live the life of the Spirit to excess. There cannot be too much love or joy or peace or goodness or kindness or self-control. The life of the Spirit is the life of freedom; no law restricts it. In the Spirit we are called beyond limits. Thus we are called beyond death to life everlasting, for only a life beyond limits can be everlastingly new and meaningful.

It is not just Paul who says that Christians should use their freedom to serve others. St. John's Gospel makes the same point in the words of Jesus himself. We have seen that it is Jesus the Messiah who sets us free; in our freedom we exercise the lordship of Christ in the world. What example of his lordship did Jesus leave us? The answer is found in the most solemn part of John's Gospel, in the beginning of Jesus' farewell discourse to his disciples at the supper he celebrated with them before his betrayal.

It was at that supper that Jesus laid aside his garments and took a towel and washed his disciples' feet. The story is so familiar that we often lose the significance it had for John's community, and which it is meant to have for us. The Gospel was written after Jesus had risen from the dead and had his messiahship proclaimed by his resurrection and ascension; thus, when he is quoted speaking to his disciples, the members of the later community heard him speaking to them as Lord of heaven and earth, seated in majesty at the right hand of the Father. As that Lord, he says, "You call me Teacher and Lord; and you are right, for so I am. If I then, your Lord and Teacher, have washed your feet, you also ought to wash one another's feet. For I have given you an example, that you also should do as I have done to you. Truly, truly, I say to you, a servant is not greater than his master; nor is he who is sent greater than he who sent him. If you know these things, blessed are you if you do them" (Jn. 13:13–17).

As Lord, Jesus serves. The servant is not greater than his master, and, as servants of the Lord, we cannot do more than serve as he served. The Greek word used for "servant" is actually the word used for "slave," to show how complete our service must be. To know the words of Jesus is one thing, but, by his own word, we are blessed in him only if we do what he did. Freedom is a way of living.

The perfection of freedom in service is one of the great paradoxes of Christian living. More accurately put, the identity of freedom and service in Jesus is not one of the Christian paradoxes, as if there were many. It is a way of stating the single Christian paradox: the identity of the power of the resurrection with the love shown on the cross. Christian power is the power of the resurrection, but that power is for love and service. We may not like it that way when we abstractly consider the Christian life from afar, but it is God's gift of love and liberation when lived.

The freedom God gives is an absolute like God himself. We must understand that freedom, like other features of the Christian life we have mentioned, is not an object to be possessed; it is the effect of God's presence in our lives. His difference sets us free. God is not subject to the limitations of time and place as we are, and when we live in him we experience time and place in a new way. Instead of time and place dominating us, his presence dominates them. That domination is our freedom in the world.

We are free because God makes us free. We were created for freedom by the word first spoken at the moment of creation, and we were later liberated from our self-inflicted captivity in time by the Word spoken as Jesus. The greatest freedom we can know is that offered to us by God in his Son. In him we do not need to pretend to be pure spirits above the world, for we are set free where we are in the world.

The liberating gift of God's presence to us springs from the resurrection of Jesus from the dead. Because God's freedom is a gift, we can receive it only where it is given. That means Christian freedom is historical through and through; it is given in time to rule time, not to escape time. It can be found only in the fleshly Jesus and the life he lived. Christian freedom is found in history, and its purpose is to make a new history. It is made available to us by Christ in the world in order to make the world the kingdom of God. Given by Jesus, freedom enables us to live for others as he did. We are free to serve.

> Lord, Jesus Christ, Son of God,
> Set me free to serve.

That is the openness to Jesus to which we are called in the Spirit. These words are, in fact, a prayer and can be said, just like the Jesus Prayer, with our breathing: the first line is said on one inhale and exhale; in the second line, "Set me free" is said on the inhale and "to serve" is said on the exhale. The prayer, so used, is a Jesus Prayer especially suited for the recognition of Jesus as Messiah.

Just as in the traditional Prayer, the lordship of Jesus is first acknowledged to be that of the Christ, the Son of God. Recognizing Jesus to be the Christ, we know that we are living in the End Time and that the mark of that time is the glorious liberty the Messiah makes available to his people. The liberty of the children of God is a sign to the world that the kingdom of God has entered the world with the Messiah's coming. Since that liberty is freedom from ourselves, it is freedom from sin, that is, freedom from serving ourselves as if we were God. Human freedom always flows from the embrace of Jesus on the cross; thus our total dependence upon God's loving mercy for the forgiveness of our sins remains at the heart of the prayer, even though different words are used than in the original Prayer.

The assurance we discovered in asking for mercy in the traditional Prayer is also found in our request for freedom in the new prayer. We ask for freedom after we have already received it. We pray to be set free in the certainty that we have already been set free, and our petition for freedom arises from the freedom given to us. If we pray, "You set me free to serve," adding the word "You" in the second line of the new form of the Prayer, we remind ourselves that our freedom has already been won for us and given to us by Christ and that our freedom is found in him alone.

We ask to be set free knowing that we have been set free. To show that it is the freedom of Jesus which frees us, we ask to be set free to serve, for the service of others is the manner in which Jesus used his freedom. We have seen that to be completely free, we must be set free from ourselves. The greatest bondage we know—sin—is self-bondage. Freed from ourselves, there are only others to serve. There is no other alternative. That is the purpose of life in the kingdom of God, for it is the way we share God's love with each other in God's way.

A further word of explanation may be helpful. When we pray, "Set me free to serve," we are not asking to be set free to serve in a sense which restricts our freedom or puts it in a kind of bondage to service. Our freedom is not, in other words, used up in service or converted into something different from it the way money is converted into something else and used up when we buy bread at the store. Instead, we are asking to be set so free that we want to serve. We ask for freedom which runs over rather than for freedom which is exhausted in a given task.

The freedom given by God is never subservient to something else; it only fulfills itself. That is what Paul meant when he said: "For freedom Christ has set us free" (Gal. 5:1). To be set free to serve and to be set free for freedom are the same for a Christian. Our freedom is God's life in us, and that life serves no master beyond itself. So it is that service in God's name is an act of love; it is totally free, required by nothing outside itself.

For a person set free in Christ, service *is* freedom. Freedom remains itself in service. Such service is joyful for the very reason that it is not compelled. To be set free for freedom means that everything done is freely done. All life is gift and that is the life of grace.

A Christian is never confronted with the situation of first being given freedom and then having to decide how to use it. We are freed from that decision in Christ. As gift from Another, our very liberation is to accept the Messiah's freedom as he gives it. Jesus' freedom is the freedom of Love to love. Such freedom is what Jesus revealed God himself to be.

To be set free to serve is to be set free in Jesus. A Christian's life is to be with Jesus, but to be with him we must be with those to whom he gave himself. He was sent to others by the Father; thus he is found only with others. Going to others, we find him, and in him we must go to others. His freedom requires others instead of being spoiled by them. How appropriate that is for freedom in the world, but how different it is from the freedom we attempt to win for ourselves by trying to shut other people out of our lives.

In Jesus our freedom depends on others in order to be itself. Service to others enables us to discover whether or not we are truly free; such service tests the reality of our freedom precisely as we have seen the reality of death tests the reality of the resurrection. Resurrection is not itself if it is not as real as death, and freedom is not itself if it is not as real as service.

Trying to use freedom for ourselves, we will demand that others serve us. Being free from ourselves, we will rejoice in serving others. There is no doubt which freedom Jesus brings. We have only to remember his words: "I am among you as one who serves" (Lk. 22:27).

If we are free, we will serve others; if we are not free, we will serve ourselves.

Service is the key to freedom, and we are set free in Christ.

A Final Word

Our concern in these pages has been to discover the nature of God's love-relationship with us in Jesus, the Messiah come to us. The recognition of God's love for us, not the repetition of a formal set of words in prayer, is the important thing. If the meaning of the Jesus Prayer, for example, is found in a person's life without using the precise words of the Prayer, it would be wrong to impose the Prayer as a rule which must be followed. We would claim, however, that a life in which the meaning of the Jesus Prayer is not found has not yet begun to be Christian.

A sequence of words can help us if we let the meaning of the words structure our lives, but a formal order of words must never be substituted for the meaning they convey. Yet that is always our temptation. We choose the words we employ, and through them we would like to control what they refer to. But if God came to us only as we wanted him when we wanted him, our relation to him would be turned upside down.

We end, then, where we began, with a reminder of the simplicity and joy of the Christian life. We must do nothing more than let God love us in Jesus, and then extend that love to others. The important thing is to recognize Jesus' presence to us as Messiah. It is not necessary for us to tell him what to do, for he comes to remake us. That means we can relax. Our first religious activity is neither ordering nor searching, but acceptance and thanksgiving. God's presence is greater than our requests, and when his presence engulfs us our requests are consumed in his perfecting love.

Our approach to God is not as important as God's approach to us; that is why recognizing God's presence in Jesus should be the principal concern of our spiritual lives. We have discovered the basic structure of our relation to God as Christians in the Jesus Prayer and the variation of it we have suggested, but those prayers, we should remember, are not means of calling God to us. They serve only as aids to help us recognize a presence which is independent of them.

When Martha had her great breakthrough concerning the identity of Jesus, she recognized him to be Lord, Christ, and Son of God. The one Jesus was all three, and it is striking that those are the same titles used of Jesus in the Jesus Prayer. When we open ourselves to God in faith and prayer, each of Martha's designations of Jesus should be given its own emphasis, and the significance of each role of Jesus should be claimed for our lives. We should from time to time pay special attention to each title, pausing after it, and letting it linger a bit longer than the others in our consciousness. The three titles supplement one another, stressing a slightly different dimension of Jesus' life which can be helpful to us on different occasions; emphasizing Jesus' nature as Lord or Christ or Son of God when we are trying to pay special attention to his presence can help us realize that he is different from us and totally independent of us. As Lord and Christ and Son of God he rules the world, and we rejoice that he calls us friends and fills us with his Spirit.

Any combination of words which enables us to recognize Jesus as God-with-us will do as a means for opening our lives to God in Christ. We need not restrict ourselves to one prayer to be used under all circumstances, even though we have been primarily concerned with but one prayer in these pages. We cannot produce God's presence mechanically. God and we are persons, and recognizing each other spontaneously in different ways in different circumstances is the way persons live together. Granting that God comes to meet us in different circumstances and under different conditions, the love he offers us is one as he is one, and his Word to us is constant; thus the underlying structure of the Christian life is unchanging in our changing world. Our spiritual lives must consequently contain marks of both stability and variableness if they are to be adequate to reality.

Although there is a oneness in the presence of the Christ to us, variations in the words we use to acknowledge his presence can add the spontaneity necessary for a living relation with God in the varied activities of our days. The variation in words need not be great to reflect the spontaneity of our lives, as we will show.

The following short prayers and reminders are only examples, but they all help express the basic structure of the Christian life we have discovered, and in doing so they show both the stability and the variety of which we have been speaking. In addition, they can all be correlated with our breathing, so that each breath we take during the day can become a reminder of God's gift to us in Christ: Father, you send your Son to me; Jesus, Lord; Lord, Jesus Christ, have mercy on me; Jesus, Lord, you are the Christ; Jesus, set me free; Jesus, mercy; Lord, Jesus, you are the Christ, the one coming into the world; Jesus, you are Lord; Jesus, fill me with your Spirit; Jesus, you are my life; Jesus, you set me free; Lord, Jesus Christ, Son of God, set me free to serve; Lord, Jesus Christ, Son of God, have mercy on me a sinner; Jesus, I live your peace; Jesus, my all; Jesus, Christ, I am set free in you; Jesus, you are my life; I live the power of the resurrection; Lord, Jesus Christ, Son of God, you set me free for freedom; Jesus, I abide in your love; Jesus, let me love in your love; Jesus, Father; Jesus . . .

We have used words to talk about words, but the most meaningful moments of our lives involve the fewest words and often no words at all. There may be times when we will find just exclaiming "Lord, Jesus" or a similar expression is prayer enough; such recognition says it all, and the lack of additional words becomes the fullness of the Spirit. Personal presence then brings us to the bursting point of words. There may be times when the presence of God so confronts us that the only prayer we can utter is "Jesus . . . Father." Then silence comes again. The Father is the ultimate Mystery and Source of all creation. No one can know him, and yet Jesus said, "He who has seen me has seen the Father" (Jn. 14:9). Jesus, the Word of God, is a mysterious Word. Jesus and the Father are one; Jesus is the Father known to us. To confront the God and Father of all through the Spirit in Jesus is our ultimate union with God. Silence then is not our experience; God is!